D0046773

Praise for *Blitz*

"David Horowitz has been rightfully standing up to crazy leftists for decades. If you're interested in debating deranged liberals with facts, you won't want to miss this latest book."

—DONALD TRUMP, JR.

"David Horowitz is one of the boldest and most brilliant thinkers and writers of our time. His latest blockbuster *Blitz* spells out why Trump will be reelected and how it will put the left in a deep sink hole of their own making. A *must* read for those who want to better understand what is really happening in the 'idea war' for the soul of America."

—GOV. MIKE HUCKABEE

"David Horowitz has written an indispensable book—*Blitz*—explaining why today's Democrats are so dangerous and why President Trump is their nemesis."

—MARK R. LEVIN, *New York Times* bestselling author of *Unfreedom of the Press*

"David Horowitz has been at the center of our national conversations about politics and culture for more than fifty years. *Blitz* is the latest must-read from Horowitz: insightful, hard-hitting, controversial, and uncompromising. Ignore him at your peril."

—PETER SCHWEIZER, *New York Times* bestselling author of *Clinton Cash* and *Profiles in Corruption*

"This book is not simply a very, very good book. It is a great book. I rarely use that term, and I read a lot of books. This is the book your anti-Trump relatives and friends should read. It is a fact-based, highly-footnoted defense of Donald Trump as president of the United States—*and* it is as clear a moral indictment of the anti-Trump left as has been written. It also has the virtues of being as clear as water and as readable as a page-turning novel. Finally, it is written by David Horowitz whom I consider a modern-day prophet. Prophets hated evil and told the truth."

—DENNIS PRAGER, President of PragerU,
New York Times bestselling author

"David Horowitz is an icon and leader in the conservative movement whose books and writings have shaped conservative policies and thinking for decades. *Blitz: Trump Will Smash the Left and Win* provides unparalleled insight into the current political climate and David's expertise and experience give him a unique understanding of how we got here and what it means for 2020 elections."

—SEAN SPICER, Host of *Spicer & Co.*, Newsmax TV

"David Horowitz hits it perfectly in this book. Horowitz understands the left better than anyone else in America. He recognizes their malevolent goals and how to stop them. This is a must read book!"

—CHARLIE KIRK, *New York Times* bestselling
author of *The MAGA Doctrine*

BLITZ

BLITZ

Trump Will Smash
the Left and Win

DAVID HOROWITZ

Humanix Books
www.humanixbooks.com

Humanix Books

Blitz
Copyright © 2020 by Humanix Books
All rights reserved

Humanix Books, P.O. Box 20989, West Palm Beach, FL 33416, USA
www.humanixbooks.com | info@humanixbooks.com

Library of Congress Cataloging-in-Publication Data is available upon request.

Humanix Books is a division of Humanix Publishing, LLC. Its trademark, consisting of the word "Humanix Books," is registered in the Patent and Trademark Office and in other countries.

ISBN: 978-163006-138-8 (Hardcover)
ISBN: 978-163006-139-5 (E-book)

Printed in the United States of America
10 9 8 7 6 5

To My Brother-in-Arms

Peter

(1939–2019)

Contents

	Preface	xi
1	The Trump Threat	1
2	Divide, Sabotage, Resist	13
3	Drain the Swamp	23
4	Identity Politics	37
5	Make America Safe	47
6	Impeachment by Any Means	61
7	America the Ugly	73
8	The Terror Caucus	89
9	Green Communism	103
10	"Equality" Versus Freedom	113
11	Trump Derangement	123
12	Impeachment by Hearsay	143
13	What the President Actually Did	161
14	The MAGA President's War	185

Afterword   203

    The Nine Biggest Dangers to America
      from the Anti-Trump Left
    The Top Ten Lies the Democrats
      Have Told You

Acknowledgments   213
Notes   215
Index   233

Preface

ON DECEMBER 18, 2019, the forty-fifth president of the United States, Donald J. Trump, was impeached by the Democrat-controlled House of Representatives. The impeachment took place a month shy of three years after Trump's inauguration in 2017, and no crime was alleged to have been committed. The vote was strictly along party lines: All House Republicans along with three Democrats voted not to impeach. Only Democrats voted to pass the two exceptionally vague articles of impeachment—"abuse of power" and "obstruction of Congress." It was the first partisan impeachment in American history.

Seven weeks later, on February 5, 2020, the U.S. Senate voted to acquit the president of the impeachment charges.

His exoneration was also the result of a party-line vote. Only one Republican senator with a history of personal grievance against the president joined the Democrat minority in seeking to remove him. The final vote was 51–49. To convict a sitting president, the Constitution requires a vote of sixty-seven senators. The fact that the vote fell so short of the constitutional requirement—an outcome predicted by all involved—underscored the unusual circumstances of this moment in American politics, and the unprecedented divisions that lay behind them. During three years of Democrat attempts to remove the president on ever-changing grounds, Americans had come to realize that their country was off course, loosed from its constitutional moorings and far from its traditional orders of business.

How far? As head of the Judiciary Committee, Representative Jerrold Nadler was one of the two principal House managers of the impeachment process in the Senate. In the heat of those hearings, Republican senators refused to support a Democrat demand about how to run the proceedings. Nadler accused them of orchestrating a "cover-up" of the president's alleged impeachable deeds. Nadler then went a momentous step further and called this opposition to a Democrat attempt to define the terms of the president's trial "obviously a treacherous vote."[1] In other words, if Republicans didn't agree with a Democrat effort to remove their president, that was *treason*.

Only twenty-one years earlier, during the impeachment of Democrat Bill Clinton, the same Jerrold Nadler had warned against precisely such partisan efforts to remove a sitting president. He called them a threat to the very fabric of

America's constitutional order: "There must never be a narrowly voted impeachment or an impeachment supported by one of our major political parties and opposed by the other. Such an impeachment . . . would produce divisiveness and bitterness in our politics for years to come and will call into question the very legitimacy of our political institutions."[2]

These were wise words. America's constitutional order, with its separation of powers and system of checks and balances, was designed to force warring factions to compromise and come together. The founders intended by these means to ensure stability and domestic peace. The fact that a prominent legislator, not to mention an entire political party, would dismiss these safeguards and pursue the very factionalism the founders feared was a disturbing indication of the dangerous waters the nation had entered.

At first glance, the candidate who emerged in 2016 should hardly have seemed a potentially divisive force. Donald Trump was a lifelong funder of liberal causes, a friend of the Clintons, a supporter of reproductive choice, an early advocate for inner-city children, a proponent of government programs and government spending. He seemed a likely figure to work with the opposing party on common interests. Yet before he ever entered the White House, the Democrats developed a hatred for Trump unprecedented in the annals of American politics. They formed a "Resistance" to his presidency, boycotted his inauguration, organized massive street demonstrations behind the slogan "Not My President," and began talking about impeaching him before he even entered the Oval Office.

In committing themselves to these uncompromising factional lines, and launching a movement to sabotage Trump's presidency, Democrats left behind half the country that had voted for him. Instead of seeking to win over the hearts and minds of Trump's supporters in the tradition of American politics, they attacked his voters as "racists," "white nationalists," "sexists," "homophobes," and "Islamophobes," and then included them in a Trump "basket of deplorables." In doing so the Democrats forged an iron bond between leader and followers. Never in American history had a president been subjected to such withering and personally vindictive attacks. When Trump's followers saw the wounds he was willing to suffer for them, they rallied to his defense.

Consequently, during the Democrats' attempts to impeach Trump as a menace to the country—"a national security threat"—his support numbers grew and grew. The day of his acquittal, Gallup reported that Trump's approval ratings had reached their highest point in his presidency.[3] Republican Party approval ratings surged dramatically as well, while Republican fund-raising was at record levels.[4] Yet Democrats persisted in their unrestrained personal attacks, apparently not grasping the fact that their unintended effect was to transform the man they called a "bully" into the perpetual victim.

Traditionally Democrats have approached politics as a form of war conducted by other means, while Republicans have entered the political arena as pragmatists and accountants. But the siege of Donald Trump has begun to create a new Republican Party, passionate and combative in defense of a leader they believe has stood up for them, and—equally important—who exceeds them in his appetite for combat.

"Populism" is the term political observers have drawn on to describe this phenomenon. The energy populism creates adds up to the *blitz* that is described in this book, and that has enabled him to overpower his opposition.

Blitz tells the story of the conflicts that define our troubling political era. It examines the sources of these political divisions, the causes of the confrontational path Democrats have chosen, and the strategic vision of a commander-in-chief willing to engage the battles and determined to win them.

. . .

As this book was in its final stages and heading for the printer, America and the world were struck by a deadly virus originating in Wuhan, China. In mid-March, as America became the nation with the most cases of the coronavirus (if you trust the Chinese statistics which I don't), Trump declared himself "a wartime president," fighting "an invisible enemy," which he described as the most dangerous enemy of all. But anyone paying attention to the political battlefield knows that there are actually two wars engulfing the country, posing dire threats to its future.

The second—visible—war was launched four years earlier by Democrats and their deep state allies to prevent Trump from being elected, then to sabotage his presidency through a vaunted "resistance," and finally to remove him from office through several failed partisan impeachment attempts. These seditious efforts are chronicled in the present book.

The first principal of psychological warfare is to attack the moral character and credibility of the adversary's commander-in-chief. If their leader is convincingly portrayed as being driven by ulterior motives that have nothing to do with the common good or winning the war, or worse as being a compulsive liar, he is effectively crippled in the task of mobilizing a united front in the war. Most people understand this, which is why there are so many calls for "unity" and working together in America's current war with the invisible enemy.

Unfortunately, the threat posed by this global pandemic has failed to cause Democrats and their anti-Trump media allies to declare a cease fire in their war to destroy the Trump presidency by destroying the man himself.

This has not only made Trump's task in leading the fight against the virus immeasurably more difficult, it has most certainly led to more cases of infection and more deaths. Readers interested in my views about the two wars can find them in an article titled "Wars Visible and Invisible," which can be accessed here: https://www.frontpagemag.com/fpm/2020/03/wars-visible-and-invisible-david-horowitz/.

The virus and its consequences will eventually be resolved. Far more ominous for the future of our country is the war described in the pages of this book.

David Horowitz
April 2020

BLITZ

1

The Trump Threat

N OVEMBER 8, 2016, WAS a day no American voter will ever
forget. For Donald Trump voters, it was a day of unex-
pected joy. For Hillary Clinton voters, it was a day of trau-
matic shock, despair, and rage.

When the polls opened, no one expected Donald Trump
to win—not even Trump himself. While the Clinton campaign had rented the vast Javits Center in New York City for
its victory celebration, the Trump campaign planned a much
smaller gathering in a modest ballroom at the New York
Hilton Midtown. Heeding the dismal news in the election-eve
polls, Trump had said, "If we're going to lose I don't want a
big ballroom."

Never again would Donald Trump believe the polls.

The *New York Times*'s *Upshot* blog calculated that Hillary had a 91 percent chance of victory. A respected political science website, the Princeton Election Consortium, confidently pegged Hillary's chances even higher: 99 percent.

That evening, as the vote-counting began, Americans across the nation attended election-night watch parties. Hillary fans were in a giddy, festive mood. Trump fans prepared themselves for bad news.

TV pundits, pollsters, and politicos reminded viewers that if Trump lost Florida (as predicted), his quest was over. Even if he won Florida, he'd be stopped by Hillary's "Blue Firewall," the states of Pennsylvania, Wisconsin, and Michigan, which no Republican presidential aspirant had won since 1988.

Early returns went as expected, with Trump winning Tennessee and West Virginia, Clinton winning Illinois and Connecticut. But in Florida, the count was surprisingly close. Across the nation, supporters of both candidates held their breath.

At 10:53 p.m. Eastern time, the networks called Florida for Trump. Twenty-one minutes later, North Carolina (which polls had leaning toward Clinton) also fell to Trump. From coast to coast, Fox News viewers whooped and high-fived while CNN viewers slumped into an anxious silence.

At the Javits Center, where Clinton supporters had assembled for Hillary's coronation, the mood was overcast. Pop icon Katy Perry took the stage to liven up the party, but she was unable to energize the stone-faced crowd.

Just after midnight, MSNBC political correspondent Kasie Hunt tweeted, "Lady Gaga is crying backstage, source reports." A few minutes later, Hunt tweeted again: "Cher is also backstage crying, source reports." A few minutes later, "Katy Perry was supposed to sing the national anthem at the Hillary Clinton victory party. Someone else took her place."

At 1:35 a.m., the networks called Pennsylvania for Trump. Among Clinton supporters, gloom turned to panic. Hillary was trailing in Wisconsin, Michigan, and Arizona. Half an hour later, Clinton campaign chairman John Podesta appeared onstage and told the funereal crowd, "They're still counting votes and every vote should count."

The networks called Wisconsin for Trump at 2:30 a.m., putting him over the top in the Electoral College. About five minutes later, Hillary Clinton called Donald Trump and conceded the election—but she didn't give a concession speech. She hadn't prepared one.

At 2:50 a.m., Donald Trump and his family took the ballroom stage. Before a jubilant crowd of supporters, he delivered a come-together speech saying, "To all Republicans and Democrats and independents across this nation, I say it is time for us to come together as one united people."

It was a gracious appeal for national unity. But the "come together" moment Trump called for would never come.

The Great Divide

Conservatives would have found it hard to get into the headspace of Hillary Clinton supporters. To them she was one of the most scandal-ridden figures in American political history, with shady dealings ranging from Whitewater and cattle futures scams to turning over America's uranium reserves to the Russians, from Clinton Foundation corruption to Benghazi betrayals, and the deletion of 33,000 subpoenaed emails. Why would anyone pin their political hopes on a presidential candidate with such baggage?

To the progressive left a Trump White House was every bit as unthinkable as a Clinton presidency to conservatives. Progressives feared—with good reason, we now know—that a Trump presidency would dismantle the "fundamental transformation" of America they thought they had put in motion during the eight years of the Obama administration. All their reforms, on the environment, on business regulation, on abortion rights, and to support a progressive future would be in jeopardy.

Trump was not only not one of them, he was their worst nightmare—disrespectful toward everything they stood for—politically *incorrect*. If they let him, Trump would set the country back decades and destroy their political dreams. Even though the election was lost, they were resolving in their hearts to stop him, and to do so by any means necessary.

Before the election result was even in, Democrats had been attacking Trump as a "racist" and "white nationalist." These characterizations were designed not just to defeat him, but to destroy him as a public figure. They were also labels that in thirty years of a successful public life had never been seriously attached to Trump, who remained a popular celebrity.

But perceiving Trump as an existential threat to their progressive dreams, Democrats and a compliant media turned to character assassination as a desperate means of stopping him. In addition to calling him a "racist," they accused him of being "mentally unstable," "incompetent," "morally disreputable," a "would-be dictator," and "unfit for the Oval office." Months before he entered the White House, leading Democrats were vowing to impeach him.

Yet Trump was able to withstand this withering barrage. More surprisingly, he was able to turn the tables on his adversaries and carry out the very agenda they feared. This political success stemmed first of all from his recognition that even though the attacks on him were personal, they were not really about him as an individual. Although the attacks on him were particularly extreme, such character-destroying slurs were not unfamiliar to Republican candidates. In fact, all of Trump's Republican predecessors had also been attacked as "racists" for challenging Democrat rule.

In the 2000 presidential campaign, the National Association for the Advancement of Colored People (NAACP) smeared George W. Bush as a racist by running ads suggesting that as governor of Texas he had condoned the gruesome dragging death of James Byrd Jr. by a couple of white skinheads. As Mona Charen reported, "though Bush signed the death warrants of the perpetrators, the NAACP, with the active collusion of then-Vice President Al Gore, spread the vile lie that Bush was somehow less than forceful in prosecuting those racist killers." In 1998, Bush had received 25 percent of the black vote in Texas. In 2000, after the NAACP ad campaign, he received 5 percent of black Texans' votes.[1]

In the 2008 campaign, Democrats smeared Republican candidate John McCain as a racist because he ran a campaign ad that juxtaposed Obama to two white women—Britney Spears and Paris Hilton—and because he had condemned Obama's mentor, Jeremiah Wright, for his anti-American rants.[2]

During the 2012 presidential campaign Obama's vice presidential running mate, Joe Biden, warned a Virginia audience with hundreds of blacks in attendance not to elect Mitt Romney and Paul Ryan because, "they're gonna put y'all back in chains."[3] At the same time, the Democratic National Committee regularly ran presidential campaign ads warning that if Republicans were elected "black churches are going to burn."[4] Racial attacks like this have been indispensable features of Democrat politics for the past half century.

Democrats have now escalated these attacks and refer regularly to Republicans and conservatives as sexists, homophobes, Islamophobes, xenophobes, and "deplorables." The point of these slanders is to stigmatize anyone who disagrees with Democrat politics as *indecent*, a proponent of "hate speech," and therefore unfit to hold public office.

Almost unique among Republican political figures, Donald Trump had a background that provided him with a certain immunity in his own mind against such attacks. He had spent most of his public life as a supporter of liberal Democrat causes. This gave him a confidence in his core values that enabled him to avoid being intimidated by leftwing attacks on his moral character, particularly the charges that he was racist, sexist, and homophobic. Because Trump was not cowed by political correctness, he could position himself as the leader of a movement to defend traditional American values, and a critic of Democrat hypocrisies.

"What the Hell Have You Got to Lose?"

Democrats ignored Trump's liberal record and slandered him as a "racist" for the same reason they laid the charge of racism at the feet of all their Republican opponents: Democrats have a scandal to hide, and stigmatizing their opponents as racists protects them. What they fear is that their political opponents will draw attention to the Democrat Party's role in the corruption, crime, and poverty that afflicts African American communities in America's inner cities. What they fear is that Republicans will challenge them in their electoral strongholds and expose the racial oppression they are responsible for.

Virtually every inner city of size in America—New York City, Detroit, Chicago, Baltimore, St. Louis, Cincinnati, Milwaukee, Newark, Atlanta—is 100 percent controlled by the Democrat Party and has been for fifty to a hundred years.[5] These cities account for the majority of the homicides and robberies in America, for the lion's share of urban poverty, welfare dependency, and drug addiction, and for a majority of the failed schools where, year in and year out, 40 percent of the students don't graduate, and 40 percent of those who do are functionally illiterate. No reforms to remedy this unconscionable situation are possible, moreover, thanks to the iron grip of Democrat teacher unions who run the schools to benefit the adults in the system rather than their student charges.

This is the dirty secret that Democrat campaigns and slanders are designed to protect. If Democrats were to lose their control of these cities, if they were to lose 20 percent or more of the black vote, they could not win another national election. Securing their one-party control of America's inner-city populations is not an option for Democrats. It is a necessity. Slandering Republicans as racists is the means by which they defend and are able to maintain the status quo.

As soon as Trump became the Republican nominee, he showed that his candidacy posed an existential threat to the Democrats' inner-city monopolies. At a campaign stop in Michigan, Trump called on African Americans, suffering under the Democrats' one-party rule, to liberate themselves by leaving the Democrat Party and voting for him. No Republican presidential candidate before him had ever done that.

"No group in America," Trump told his audience, "has been more harmed by [Democrat] policies than African Americans. No group. No group. If [the Democrats'] goal was to inflict pain on the African American community, [they] could not have done a better job. It's a disgrace.

"Tonight, I'm asking for the vote of every African American citizen in this country who wants to see a better future. Look how much African American communities have suffered under Democratic control. To those I say the following: 'What do you have to lose by trying something new, like Trump? . . . You're living in poverty. Your schools are no good. You have no jobs. Fifty-eight percent of your youth is unemployed. What the hell do you have to lose?'

"America must reject the bigotry of [the Democrats,] who see communities of color only as votes, not as human beings worthy of a better future. . . . [Democrats] would rather provide a job to a refugee from overseas than to give that job to unemployed African American youth in cities like Detroit, who have become refugees in their own country."[6]

It was a devastating indictment—and irrefutable. Recognizing this, Democrats made no effort to answer the charge with facts. Instead they resorted to the response they had perfected over decades, stigmatizing Trump as a racist. In effect, they said, "Don't listen to Trump. He's a *white supremacist* whose goal is to deny African American success, emphasize African American failure, and scare white people with the threat of black violence and out-of-control crime."

In its coverage of Trump's speech, the *Detroit News* included an interview with a local black pastor, which showed the efficacy of this tactic. When the *News* asked, "What do you have to lose?" the pastor said: "We have *everything* to lose by voting for him. This man is a bigot."[7] He then reeled off various racial and ethnic slurs the Democrats had already marshaled to demonize Trump.

In 2018, the same leftist counterattack became the subject of a book by Pulitzer Prize–winning author Juan Williams. It was called: *What The Hell Do You Have to Lose?: Trump's War on Civil Rights*. Williams delivered the Democrat party line: "[Trump] wants to see black failure and misery. That view justifies his distaste for black people—some might say his racism. He locks his eyes on the worst of black American life because it makes him and other white people into victims of the trouble in black neighborhoods; he is the hero defending whites against the approaching barbarians."[8]

Of course, Trump never said anything about defending whites or making them the victims of the trouble in black neighborhoods. He addressed his speech entirely to black victims of what were essentially racist leftist policies. Far from displaying "distaste" for black people, he was showing concern and compassion for them. Far from being a racist, Trump was responsible for many acts of compassion for African Americans. In May 2018, to take one example,

Trump issued a posthumous pardon for boxing champion Jack Johnson, a black man convicted by an all-white jury in 1913 on a contrived "morals" charge. It was an injustice that a dozen presidents, including Barack Obama, had failed to correct.

Juan Williams's anti-Trump animus caused him to accuse Trump—without any evidence—of wanting to deny the revolution in race relations that had taken place in his lifetime, and the tremendous successes of black America over the last half century. "The country still has a long way to go before approaching racial equality," wrote Williams, "but the revolution in race relations during the last fifty years—the majority of Donald Trump's life—has been absolutely mind-boggling. Instead of asking black people what they have to lose by voting for him, Trump needs to ask himself, 'How the hell did I miss all of this?'"[9]

This argument was based on no actual evidence that Trump had failed to notice the Civil Rights Revolution. At this particular moment in time when Democrats and leftists were constantly denigrating America as a "white supremacist country" and claiming falsely that the nation's true heritage was racism and slavery, conservatives were constantly reminding progressives that America is defined by its dedication to equality and freedom—never perfect but always advancing. In other words, conservatives were constantly *drawing attention to* the "absolutely mind-boggling revolution that had taken place in race relations over the last fifty years."

One might well ask Juan Williams: "Instead of berating Trump, and denying his efforts to raise up the millions of blacks left behind in America's inner cities, why aren't you reaching out to him to test his sincerity? Why aren't you con-fronting the anti-white and anti-American radicals in your own party, which include such prominent leaders as Cory Booker and Beto O'Rourke, who maliciously portray America as a nation defined by its worst moments instead of its best?"

Kanye West at the White House

Of course it was no mystery why Williams didn't confront the Bookers, O'Rourkes, and other denigrators of America and Trump in his own party. Or why he made no effort to reach out to Trump and test his sincerity. Kanye West— African American rapper, fashion designer, and icon to the black community, had indeed made such an effort. He donned a "Make America Great Again" Trump hat and vis-ited the White House, where he helped secure Trump's sup-port for the First Step Act of prison reform. He persuaded Trump to lobby for the bill's passage in the Senate. Trump signed it into law on December 21, 2018. While the First Step Act resulted in the freeing of thousands of black prisoners, a reform long on the wish list of the African American com-munity, the left's response to West's outreach to Trump was ridicule and worse.

A typical piece in ESPN's online magazine *The Undefeated* reported West's White House visit this way: "Last week, we didn't get the Kanye West who spoke up for us. We got some-thing unfamiliar, terrifying and ignorant. We got a West with 'Make America Great Again' hats. . . . He's been calling Trump a genius. . . . We got an unending vomit-like array of misin-formation. But maybe that's the Kanye West we should have seen coming for a long time."[10]

CNN's Trump-hating black anchor Don Lemon chimed in with this: "What I saw was a minstrel show today. Him in front of all these white people embarrassing himself and embarrassing Americans, but mostly African Americans because every one of them is sitting either at home or with their phones, watching this, cringing. I couldn't even watch it. I had to turn the television off because it was so hard to watch. Him sitting there, being used by the president of the United States."[11]

The Kanye-Trump meeting was a historic event, creating a bridge between a Republican White House and America's forgotten black communities. It laid the groundwork for needed help to America's inner cities and for the reform of America's treatment of blacks in prison. But instead of celebrating the achievement, progressives turned Kanye's triumph into Kanye's crucifixion. It was an effective warning to other blacks, including Juan Williams, not to break ranks and try the same.

2

Divide, Sabotage, Resist

FIVE DAYS AFTER THE 2016 election, a closed-door meeting took place in the nation's capital at the luxurious Mandarin Oriental Hotel. The purpose of the meeting was first to plot a formal Resistance to the new president, and second to adopt a strategy for moving the Democratic Party further to the political left. The entire event was organized and paid for by George Soros's "Democracy Alliance."

The Alliance is a coalition of 110 billionaires who have each pledged to contribute $200,000 a year toward leftwing causes. For decades, Soros has worked to shape the politics of the Democratic Party by creating a coalition of leftwing groups that will support his agendas. The coalition consists of trade unions, political movements like the Marxoid "Working

Families Party," philanthropic and advocacy groups like the Tides Foundation, blacklist organizations and smear sites like Blood Money and the Southern Poverty Law Center, and violent street communists who fomented anti-capitalist protests and anti-police riots, like "Occupy Wall Street" and "Black Lives Matter."[12]

The Mandarin Oriental gathering lasted four days. Among its attendees were several hundred activists and politicians like House Democratic leader Nancy Pelosi, Senator Elizabeth Warren, and Congressional Progressive Caucus co-chairman Keith Ellison. According to the *Politico* reporter who was present at the meeting, "Some sessions deal with gearing up for 2017 and 2018 elections, while others focus on thwarting President-elect Trump's 100-day plan, which the agenda calls 'a terrifying assault on President Obama's achievements—and our progressive vision for an equitable and just nation.'" Commented the reporter: "If the agenda is any indication, liberals plan full-on trench warfare against Trump from Day One."[13]

The Resistance army was composed of 172 organizations, among which a group calling itself "Indivisible" was one of the major players. An online handbook for the troops published by Indivisible summarized the movement's vision: "Donald Trump is the biggest popular-vote loser in history to ever call himself President. In spite of the fact that he has no mandate, he will attempt to use his congressional majority to reshape America in his own racist, authoritarian, and corrupt image. If progressives are going to stop this, we must stand indivisibly opposed to Trump and the members of Congress who would do his bidding. Together, we have the power to resist—and we have the power to win."[14]

It was a declaration of war.

Launching the Resistance

The first action of the anti-Trump forces that Soros had marshaled took place the day after Trump's inauguration. The action was organized by "The Women's March," led by anti-Israel activist and terrorist supporter Linda Sarsour. It was the largest demonstration in U.S. history, involving several million activists in 600 cities. They marched behind the slogan "Not My President," and accused Trump of being racist, sexist, and anti-immigrant. A memorable point of the afternoon was a speech by the aging pop star Madonna, who told the cheering activists, "I've thought an awful lot about blowing up the White House."[15]

The most striking feature of the Resistance and its rejection of a legitimately elected president was its departure from the political tradition established by the constitutional framers over 230 years earlier. The most pressing fear of those framers was the threat that political factions posed to a democracy. They were conscious of the fact that historically, democracies such as classical Athens had split into rival factions that eventually tore them apart and led to their demise. To prevent this outcome, the framers constructed a political order featuring structural "checks and balances," which were designed to frustrate divisive ambitions. These included institutions like the Electoral College, created with the specific goal of forcing factions to compromise with their opponents and moderate their ambitions.

Over the years, a tradition had developed to further the goals of compromise and moderation. Referred to as "the presidential honeymoon," this tradition was a period of time following an election when the opposition party allowed the new president to get in place, confirm his cabinet, and float his legislative agenda. According to the Gallup organization, presidential honeymoons have lasted an average of seven months in recent years. Barack Obama's lasted even longer.[16] The presidential honeymoon furthered the framer's goals of encouraging compromise, creating a "loyal opposition," and ensuring stability in the body politic. But thanks to the anti-Trump Resistance strategy devised by Soros and the left, there was no honeymoon for Donald Trump.

In an unprecedented act of defiance, 70 sitting Democratic members of Congress boycotted the Trump inauguration. This was followed by the most acrimonious confirmation hearings in living memory, as several of Trump's cabinet nominees were accused of being "racists" by Democratic senators—with no credible evidence to back up the charges. A prime example was Trump's nominee for U.S. Attorney General, Senator Jeff Sessions, who had previously desegregated Alabama's public schools as the state's attorney general, and also prosecuted the Ku Klux Klan for a racial murder. Not even senate collegiality protected Sessions from being attacked as a racist by senators Blumenthal and Booker who had served with Sessions and were voicing this baseless and destructive accusation for the first time.

As one writer for *Real Clear Politics* observed of the Democrats' break with tradition: "The honeymoon period is an important social tradition for personal relationships as well as political interactions. Judgments are supposed to be suspended, or at least held in reserve, as a way to give the new arrangement a chance to work. A businessman with no prior political experience needs this span of saving grace more than most. Our country would have been better served if Trump's detractors, out of respect for the office of the president, held their bitter feelings in abeyance while the new leader was allowed to get his sea legs."[17]

But the explicit *purpose* of the Resistance strategy was to prevent the new leader from getting his "sea legs" or giving "the new arrangement a chance to work." Calling it a Resistance could not help but conjure images of the Resistance to the Nazi occupation in Europe during World War II. The word connotes obstruction and sabotage—an all-out effort to prevent the agenda of an "illegitimate" president and his deplorable supporters from being implemented.

The contrast between Donald Trump's "America First," "Make America Great Again" populism—his efforts to protect America's borders and revive the economy—and the intractable partisan Resistance mounted by the Democrats could not have been starker. On one side was Trump's patriotism, his desire to rally Americans behind their country. On the other was the partisan factionalism of the Democrats, their objection to the election result and dismissive contempt for Trump and the 63 million Americans who voted for him.

The So-Called Muslim Ban

The Democrats' Resistance strategy was explicitly designed to obstruct the president's agenda and foster divisive factionalism. Its impact was felt immediately. One of Trump's earliest initiatives was an executive order instituting a "temporary ban" or moratorium on immigration from six Middle Eastern countries that were either failed states where there was no central authority or state sponsors of terror. The president's concern was that these governments could not provide reliable vetting of those emigrating from their countries and therefore could not render a trustworthy opinion as to whether or not they were terrorists.

Trump took the six countries from a list the Obama administration had used to institute a similar moratorium. As it happened the six countries were Muslim. The Resistance seized on this fact to attack Trump as "anti-Muslim"—a religious bigot and a racist.

In the words of a leftist political science professor, this is how Trump's temporary moratorium on immigration from terrorist countries and failed states was met by the anti-Trump forces: "Soon after taking office, Trump issued an executive order limiting travel from six predominantly Muslim countries. Immediately, a coalition of religious, immigrant rights, and labor groups led a campaign to fight back. Spontaneously [sic!], they protested at airports, filed lawsuits, and then persuaded dozens of universities and churches, mayors of big cities, and California's political leaders, to resist cooperation with the federal crackdown. Several federal courts [also ideologically aligned with the Resistance] blocked Trump's ban, stopping the president from carrying out one of his top campaign promises."[18]

Another way of viewing this is to call it what it was: a deceptive and seditious revolt, whose effect was to endanger American citizens.

Responding to his critics, Trump appealed to common sense and the common interest: "This is not about religion. This is about terror and keeping our country safe. There are over 40 different countries worldwide that are majority Muslim that are not affected by this order." Trump then encapsulated his message in a signature slogan designed to appeal to all Americans: "Make America Safe Again."[19]

An Unforeseen Consequence

In waging their battles against the president's initiative, Democrats and their media allies ignored Trump's common-sense defense of American interests and continued to characterize the moratorium as an "anti-Muslim ban," though it was neither anti-Muslim nor a permanent "ban." The label allowed the Resistance to attack Trump as an "anti-Muslim racist." Even then the charge was woven out of whole cloth on the grounds that Muslims were "brown" and Trump was influenced by this and therefore a bigot. This slander was endlessly repeated despite the hundreds of thousands of brown-skinned immigrants who were admitted legally every year into the United States by the Trump administration from countries that included the 51 Muslim nations that were not part of the president's proposed moratorium.

Instead of retreating in the face of the false accusations, Trump continued to emphasize the rationale for his policy—the security and safety of all Americans. In other words, the American family—a collectivity the Democrats seemed to have forgotten—against the external threats it faced.

As their opposition progressed, it became apparent that the resisters' strategy was producing an unintended consequence, affecting the political war with the president and his supporters that followed. Instead of focusing on the *issues*, the Democrats' decision to demonize the *man* forced them to take harder policy positions than they might otherwise have chosen, severely narrowing their options in the process.

A major conflict, for example, was immigration policy itself, and, specifically, Trump's campaign promise to complete the wall on America's southern border. Previous administrations, both Democrat and Republican, had started building the wall, but left it incomplete. If the Democrats' focus had been on Trump's policies rather than his person, if they had not been so intent on stigmatizing him as a "racist," they could have found some common ground. They probably wouldn't have opposed his funding requests for strengthening and extending the existing wall entirely, as they actually did. After all, Democrats had readily supported similar funding requests for the wall from President Obama.

But their hatred for Trump, and determination to resist him, forced them into defending what was in effect an "open borders" policy, which they had previously not supported. The same circumstance forced them to support the attacks on the border by their hard left members, who were calling U.S. Immigration and Customs Enforcement (ICE) border guards a "Gestapo," and the ICE detention centers "concentration camps."

On the one hand, this was an explicit agenda of the Soros coalition: to push the Democratic Party further toward the left and away from the more reasonable positions the party had held until then. The results of this push were evident in the radicalism manifested by Democratic primary contenders who soon wanted to "decriminalize" illegal border crossings and provide government health care to people who broke the law to enter the country. This new radicalism promised to have a significant impact on the Democrats' prospects in the 2020 election.

It could have been different. During the Obama years, Democrats had supported the border wall as a national security imperative. Now their leader Nancy Pelosi was claiming that "a wall is an immorality"—a transparent absurdity.[20] Pelosi and the Democrats topped this by calling the wall racist. Theirs was a desperate position that lacked even a semblance of plausibility and could only be supported as an attack on Trump.

The strategy of blocking Trump at all costs left Democrats vulnerable to a voting public that was not persuaded by this strange logic and was unable to disregard the threat posed by unvetted illegals crossing the border, carrying unknown contagious diseases and with undisclosed criminal records.

By demonizing Trump, the Democrats had forced themselves into the position of being the "Party of No," a stance they would not have chosen in other circumstances. Democrats' political options were severely narrowed by the decision to demonize Trump in other areas as well. For example, traditionally they had been strong advocates of "infrastructure investment" not least because it would feed their union constituencies. Trump was a natural partner for such a program because he was a builder and lacked the traditional conservative qualms about spending government money. It was a promising setup for a bipartisan deal. But the Democrats could not make deals with Trump on what had become divisive issues; they could not afford "to give Trump a win." It would be a pact with the devil and undermine the Resistance.

The determination to stigmatize and obstruct a legitimately elected president was irreversible. It would play a central role in making the years following the 2016 election the most bitterly divisive since the Civil War.

3

Drain the Swamp

JUST SEVEN MONTHS INTO the Trump presidency, journalist Thomas Frank summed up the mainstream media's attitude toward the new president in these words: "The news media's alarms about Trump have been shrieking at high C for more than a year. It was in January of 2016 [a year before Trump's inauguration] that the *Huffington Post* began appending a denunciation of Trump as a 'serial liar, rampant xenophobe, racist, birther and bully' to every single story about the man. It was last August that the *New York Times* published an essay approving of the profession's collective understanding of Trump as a political mutation—an unacceptable deviation from the two-party norm—that journalists must cleanse from the political mainstream."

Far from dissenting from these fevered attacks, Frank embraced them: "Trump certainly has it coming. He is obviously incompetent, innocent of the most basic knowledge about how government functions. His views are repugnant. His advisers are fools. He appears to be dallying with obviously dangerous forces"—a reference to unfounded Democrat accusations that Trump was a Russian agent or—to quote MSNBC anchor Rachel Maddow's unhinged commentary—"the American presidency is effectively a Russian op."[21]

These reckless media smears were completely detached from the reality of Trump's accomplishments in his first seven months. His tax and deregulation policies had created a record-setting economy. Unemployment rates for minorities had reached historic lows. He had strengthened the North Atlantic Treaty Organization (NATO) and even shattered the leftist claims of a Trump-Russia collusion when he punished Putin's murderous ally Bashar al-Assad with a devastating Tomahawk missile strike. Trump was also well on his way to destroying the Islamic caliphate in eight months—something Barack Obama had failed to accomplish with five years of feeble military efforts.

The bizarre and baseless media attacks on the president were intended to halt Trump's progress and shake the loyalty of his 63 million political supporters. Instead, Trump continued to rack up policy victories, while the media attacks actually intensified his public support.

Trump's Twitter Feed

No aspect of Trump's presidency has been more widely criticized than his rhetorical barbs, especially on the social media site Twitter. Though Barak Obama was the first president to use Twitter, Trump mastered the art of the tweet as a means of communicating directly to his constituencies without the filter of a hostile press.

On June 4, 2017, for example, after the deadly Islamic terror attack on London Bridge, Trump tweeted, "We must stop being politically correct and get down to the business of security for our people. If we don't get smart it will only get worse." Trump's critics in the media claimed he should have limited his remarks to condolences for the people of London. But Trump wasn't about to hide the fact that the politically correct effort to protect the Islamic world from accountability for the deeds of its radical elements had led to a dramatic weakening of the West's defenses.

A month later, Trump's media critics roared their disapproval when he retweeted a ten-year-old video of a Trump appearance on WWE's WrestleMania. The video had been altered so that when Trump, dressed in a suit and tie, appeared to body slam a man outside the ring, his victim's face was covered by the CNN logo. It was clever political satire, and Trump retweeted it shortly before the Sunday TV talk shows for maximum impact. Trump knew the talking heads would condemn it—but his supporters would applaud a body slam of the media. Hashtagged #FraudNewsCNN, it was one of the most retweeted of all Trump's posts.

The media also did a collective spit-take over a November 11, 2017, Trump tweet. The president responded to a statement by North Korean dictator Kim Jong-un that called Trump a "lunatic old man." Trump's well-crafted response: "Why would Kim Jong-un insult me by calling me 'old,' when I would

NEVER call him 'short and fat?' Oh well, I try so hard to be his friend—and maybe someday that will happen!" Pundits excoriated Trump for insulting the Communist dictator instead of attempting to negotiate with him. Seven months later, in June 2018, Trump and Kim greeted each other warmly at their first summit in Singapore, which elicited derisive remarks from the same media that had criticized him before.

On January 20, 2018, just before the second Women's March protest against him, he struck just the right note of sarcastic congratulation, while touting his administration's triumphs on behalf of women: "Beautiful weather all over our great country, a perfect day for all Women to March. Get out there now to celebrate the historic milestones and unprecedented economic success and wealth creation that has taken place over the last 12 months. Lowest female unemployment in 18 years!"

The leftist media could never understand why Trump would praise dictators like Vladimir Putin, Recep Erdoğan, Kim Jong-un, and Xi Jinping. But Trump had always made deals by building relationships with the people across the table. That approach resulted in tweets like this one from April 8, 2018: "President Xi and I will always be friends, no matter what happens with our dispute on trade. China will take down its Trade Barriers because it is the right thing to do. Taxes will become Reciprocal & a deal will be made on Intellectual Property. Great future for both countries!" Heads exploded at CNN and MSNBC, but this tweet helped keep China at the bargaining table.

A tweet's brevity forces blunt discourse. Trump's "in your face" tweets do not reflect a lack of knowledge about how government should function, as his critics both left and right maintain. Rather, they are a calculated strategy to blow back the bullies of political correctness and political doublespeak, who had effectively cowed Republicans through the previous two administrations. The purpose of bluntness is precisely its shock value, which changes the dynamics of a political exchange, peels back its deceptions, and—in a favorite trope of the left—"speaks truth to power."

Deferring to Hillary Clinton as a female, as Republicans prior to Trump had done, allowed her to hide behind a veil of gentility while she launched a one-woman witch hunt against them, calling Republicans racists, sexists, deplorables, and so on. It took a Trump to look her in the eye with seventy million people watching during one of the presidential debates and say, "You are a liar and a crook," which she was both. Everybody knew it, but only Donald Trump dared to utter it out loud.

Long before Twitter was created, Trump had made it clear that if such a means ever became available it would suit him perfectly. In his book *The America We Deserve*, written seventeen years before his presidential run, Trump explained his attitude toward political speech: "Most politicians use language to conceal what they think. Or to conceal the fact that they don't think. Many are trained as lawyers and use language to win support rather than to define the truth. Being blunt hasn't hurt me so far. I use language to speak my mind. I've lived my life as I choose, and said what I wanted to say."[22]

Trump's blunt candor won the support of the working and middle classes who had grown increasingly frustrated by politics-as-usual. They had seen slick politicians of both parties vow to serve the people and the Constitution, then go to Washington and serve themselves and special interests. Both Republicans and Democrats had promised for thirty years, for example, to solve the problem of border security and illegal immigration. By the 2016 election, the voters had figured out that both parties viewed the border crisis as an issue to run on, not an issue to solve. Then along came Trump, speaking his mind, bluntly and forcefully, vowing to build a wall and "Make America Safe Again."

Once elected, President Trump gored the oxen of the left on a daily basis, and they responded by attacking him. Even Trump's conservative supporters were sometimes uncomfortable with his blunt-force tweets. What Trump's critics on the right failed to appreciate was that his unapologetic refusal to genuflect before PC sacred cows had an explosive—and long-overdue—impact on the progressive culture. The PC culture with its leftist bias had dominated political discourse in the decades since the radical sixties. No one but Trump had the audacity to reshape that discourse.

By frankly saying what needs to be said regardless of conventional decorum, Trump regularly lights up the media with his tweets. His leftist critics cry foul and accuse him of being an obsessive narcissist or of not being sufficiently "presidential." His supporters on the right sometimes cringe at his tweets and complain that he often steps on his own message. But both left and right miss the point.

Trump ascended to the office as an apprentice politician. He had to feel his way under intense and hostile media scrutiny. He was being aggressively sabotaged by agents of the deep state. In this difficult environment, Trump certainly made mistakes. But even as an apprentice, Trump wielded his Twitter account as a potent weapon against his ideological opponents. Trump's abrasiveness often provoked them to overreact and expose their partisan agenda and dishonesty. In this way, Trump shone a spotlight into the deep chasm in the nation's politics. Through his tweets—and the overreactions of his enemies—Trump proved that the problem in America is not a character issue in the White House, but a deep ideological rift that has been tearing at the fabric of American life for decades.

An Illuminating Case

One such combustion occurred on July 27, 2019, when a Trump tweet vented the president's ire at Congressman Elijah Cummings, the African American chair of the Government Oversight Committee. The president was angry with Cummings for a humiliating dressing-down of Trump's acting secretary of Homeland Security, Kevin McAleenan, over conditions in migrant camps along the border. McAleenan had been summoned to testify about the crisis caused by the flood of migrants seeking illegal entry into the United States. He only got to say eight words—"We're doing our level best in a challenging . . ."—when Cummings interrupted and launched into a two-minute tirade.

Cummings's Democrat colleagues had already compared the migrant camps to Auschwitz, so the leftists' rhetoric had already bottomed out at the *reductio ad Hitlerum* level. Cummings took full advantage of the protection afforded by the rules of political correctness, which protected African Americans like him. He scolded and berated McAleenan as if he were a delinquent child, confident that no one would dare criticize him. Clenching his fist and leaning into the microphone, Cummings shouted, "What does that mean? What does that mean when a child is sitting in their own feces, can't take a shower? Come on, man. What's that about? None of us would have our children in that position. They are human beings."[23] In other words you're a racist who treats brown people as though they were less than human.

Personally insulted by this treatment of his cabinet secretary, and outraged by the left's attacks on America's border guards who risked their lives to defend American citizens, the president exploded in a tweet: "Rep. Elijah Cummings has been a brutal bully, shouting and screaming at the great men & women of Border Patrol about conditions at the Southern Border, when actually his Baltimore district is FAR WORSE and more dangerous."[24]

Nor was Trump finished. In his next tweet, he wrote: "As proven last week during a Congressional tour, the Border is clean, efficient & well run, just very crowded. Cummings' District is a disgusting, rat and rodent infested mess. If he spent more time in Baltimore, maybe he could help clean up this very dangerous & filthy place."[25]

The left came unglued. Trump had dared to criticize a black man—so he was, ipso facto, a racist. House Judiciary Committee chair Jerrold Nadler told ABC-TV: "Well, the president is as he usually is often is disgusting and racist."[26] House Speaker Nancy Pelosi tweeted: "We all reject racist attacks against [Rep. Cummings] and support his steadfast leadership."[27]

Senator Joe Biden, the leading contender at the time for the Democratic nomination, addressed Trump directly: "It is despicable for you to attack him and the people of Baltimore this way. Once again you have proved yourself unfit to hold the office. A President is supposed to lift this nation up. Not tear it down."

Washington State Governor Jay Inslee, also a 2020 contender, said: "Donald Trump . . . is just a racist who lives in the White House."[28] Connecticut Senator Chris Murphy announced: "I'm unfollowing the President of the United States today on Twitter, because his feed is the most hate-filled, racist, and demeaning of the 200+ I follow, and it regularly ruins my day to read it. So I'm just going to stop."[29]

Speaking in the name of black America, the Chairman of the NAACP pronounced a summary judgment: "The vile racist attack on Congressman Elijah Cummings and the City of Baltimore is despicable. The White House is the seat of a criminal enterprise and a racist cesspool."[30]

This partisan uproar revealed the central paradox of Trump's presidency. It showed how, by standing up to the attacks from the left, Trump was able to thrive despite their slanderous labels of "racist" and "hate monger." It's inconceivable that, say, Paul Ryan or Jeb Bush would have stood their ground against the "racist" smears. They would have been steamrolled by the viciousness of the left and quickly apologized for any "offense" given.

Trump's response illustrated a basic strategy that has served him well on the political battlefield: When attacked, strike back. Strike back hard. Harder than they hit you. Use the facts concealed by political correctness, and the language of moral indictment, which progressives resort to all the time. Know that there are many millions of Americans who have been intimidated into silence by the same tactics, who will rally to your defense.

Donald Trump never attacked the people of Baltimore. Instead, he accurately diagnosed the political pathology that kept the people of Baltimore trapped in poverty and dependence. Whatever his intentions, Elijah Cummings had failed his own people. He was part of the swamp in D.C. Donald Trump was committed to draining that swamp, and he weaponized Twitter to serve that end.

How Low Would the Anti-Trumpers Go?

The anti-Trump chorus seized on Trump's use of the word "infested" (as in "rodent and drug-infested") claiming it proved Trump's racism. Chris Matthews, host of *Hardball* on MSNBC, went on a rant: "Infested, infested, infested . . . It's a word . . . It's vermin, it's a Hitlerian term. You go back and read Goebbels and all that stuff, it's all about the Jews in that case. It's the use of the word vermin—infested, he's obsessed with this thing, about cities."[31]

Any other Republican would have backed down in the face of this onslaught and found a way to distance himself from his own remarks. But Trump was not a prisoner of the PC culture that fueled the hate against him. Instead of apologizing, Trump posted a video of Cummings using the same word—"infested"—to describe his own Baltimore community. He had done so at a congressional hearing twenty years earlier: "This morning, I left my community of Baltimore—a drug-infested area, where a lot of the drugs that we're talking about today have already taken the lives of so many children—the same children that I watched 14 or 15 years ago as they grew up now walking around like zombies."[32]

The PC rules of engagement were both unmistakable and indefensible: If a white Republican criticized a black Democrat—or worse, took him to the woodshed—*that* constituted "disgusting," "racist" behavior regardless of his intentions or whether the facts supported his criticism. If a white Republican demonstrated concern over intolerable conditions in a black-run inner city, that constituted a racist attack on the city and its inhabitants. This line of reasoning is not about helping the inner city or its poor minorities. It's about damning conservatives if they do or if they don't, by smearing them as selfish, mean-spirited "white supremacists." It's about maintaining an unconscionable and oppressive status quo.

Does this sound like a caricature of "liberal" opinion? Here is the editorial comment of the sophisticated, liberal *New Yorker* on Trump's tweet against the deplorable conditions in Baltimore's inner city: "'No human being would want to live there,' Trump said of Baltimore on Twitter, implicitly questioning the humanity of the six hundred thousand human beings who do, in fact, live there."[33]

This nasty absurdity was actually outdone by the editors of the liberal *Baltimore Sun*, whose editorial headline *defended the rats* in order to condemn the president: "Better to Have a Few Rats Than to Be One."[34] Actually, it's not a few rats from which Baltimore's poorest neighborhoods suffer. A year previously, the pest-control company Orkin listed Baltimore as the ninth most rat-infested city in America (Democrat-run Chicago is number one).[35] What the *Baltimore Sun* editorialists were actually defending with their repellent headline was their own collusion in creating the disgraceful state of the city they were supposed to be looking out for.

Behind the Hate

Baltimore *is* a mess, just as Trump claimed. Moreover, its decline can be traced to the moment over fifty years earlier when the city became a Democrat monopoly.[36] Baltimore's decline has been so precipitous under a half century of Democratic rule that it has lost more than 30 percent of its population.[37] Today Baltimore ranks as the fourth most dangerous city in America with a violent crime rate that is more than five *times* the national average, murder and robbery rates that are nearly 12 *times* the national average, and a 22 percent poverty rate, which is nearly twice the national figure.[38]

Baltimore's failed school system spends a third more per pupil than the national average while less than 12 percent of the students from fourth grade through high school qualify as proficient in math. Yet thousands of individuals—consultants, contractors, and administrators—are paid in excess of $100,000 a year to perpetrate this travesty.[39] And because these employees are protected by Democratic unions whose priorities are the dues-paying adults, not the children, they can't be fired.

Of course, Baltimore does have wealthy neighborhoods, as Cummings's defenders were quick to point out. But "social justice" Democrats like Cummings habitually counsel others to judge governments by how they treat the most vulnerable of their inhabitants not the most powerful and prosperous. By that standard Baltimore is a much worse mess than the temporary situation at the border that triggered Cummings's moral ire and precipitated his attack on the acting secretary and his border patrol.

When Cummings passed away in October 2019, *Boston Herald* columnist Don Feder described him as "typical of the political class":

> Yesterday, Elijah Cummings—chairman of the powerful House Oversight and Reform Committee—ascended to that big welfare state in the sky. The man who represented Maryland's 7th Congressional District for 23 years is being lionized as a champion of the downtrodden.
>
> Along with 14 years in the Maryland legislature, Mr. Cummings spent nearly 4 decades in the cozy bosom of government, almost all of his adult life. His net worth is variously estimated at between $1.3 million and $1.5 million—modest compared to some members of Congress, but far exceeding the average in his district, which has an unemployment rate of 13.4%—roughly four times the national average. Cummings district is one of the poorest, most dilapidated, most dismal in the country. While the people he represented live in squalor, the Congressman made headlines and lived handsomely.[40]

Who is to blame for the violence, poverty, poor sanitation, and educational malpractice that afflicts inner-city Baltimore? Who else *is* there to blame but Baltimore's unaccountable Democrat machine that runs the city without any meaningful opposition? In 2018 over $21 billion in federal dollars were given to Baltimore, $15.7 billion of which went to Cummings's own district. Where did the money go? Into whose pockets?[41] The Democrats and their leftist ideology created Baltimore's misery, and they own it. For decades, Elijah Cummings benefited politically from the corrupt system that dominated Baltimore. The people Cummings represented were no better off at the end of his tenure than when he took office. As Donald Trump accurately pointed out, many of Cummings's constituents live in far worse conditions than the people in the migrant camps on the border.

Trump knew he would be branded a racist, but he didn't shrink from the fight. Instead, he applied the same standard to Democrats that Cummings had applied to Republicans: "If racist Elijah Cummings would focus more of his energy on helping the good people of his district, and Baltimore itself, perhaps progress could be made in fixing the mess that he has helped to create over many years of incompetent leadership. His radical 'oversight' is a joke!"[42]

Before Trump, no Republican leader would have called a black Democrat like Elijah Cummings "racist." No other Republican would have dared accuse Cummings of being responsible for the misery of his constituents. But in defying political correctness, Trump applied a single standard to blacks and whites. In so doing, he deprived progressives of their moral cover for deplorable misdeeds. It was essential to exposing the reality that everyone is aware of but afraid to mention. That is how Trump has become such a transformative and polarizing leader since he entered the White House.

4

Identity Politics

FOR DARING TO CRITICIZE Elijah Cummings and for stating the truth about the appalling conditions in Cummings's district, Donald Trump's foes branded him "racist." Yet Trump's concern for the plight of inner-city minorities was genuine. He didn't discover the issue during his dustup with Cummings. From his 2000 book *The America We Deserve* to his inaugural address on January 20, 1917, Trump had been consistent in drawing attention to inner-city poverty, crime, and wretched schools.

Whereas Trump's predecessors owed their allegiance to political machines, political elites, and special interests, Trump proposed himself as a new populist voice who represented the people—especially the forgotten people. "Today," he said in his inaugural address, "we are not merely transferring power from one Administration to another, or from one party to another—but we are transferring power from Washington, D.C., and giving it back to you, the American People."

This was the central theme of Trump's campaigns, and therefore his battles with his Democrat opponents. "For too long," Trump explained in the same address, "a small group in our nation's Capital has reaped the rewards of government, while the people have borne the cost. . . . Washington flourished—but the people did not share in its wealth. Politicians prospered—but the jobs left, and the factories closed."

Trump then described the aspirations of the voting public that the political class had betrayed: "Americans want great schools for their children, safe neighborhoods for their families, and good jobs for themselves. These are the just and reasonable demands of a righteous public. But for too many of our citizens, a different reality exists: Mothers and children trapped in poverty in our inner cities; rusted-out factories scattered like tombstones across the landscape of our nation; an education system, flush with cash, but which leaves our young and beautiful students deprived of knowledge; and the crime and gangs and drugs that have stolen too many lives and robbed our country of so much unrealized potential."

In conclusion, Trump pledged: "This American carnage stops right here and stops right now."[43]

Defending the Indefensible

The left pounced on the phrase "American carnage" to twist the words of the speech into its own anti-Trump narrative. Commenting on the inauguration, *Washington Post* senior editor Marc Fisher excoriated Trump: "Never before had an American president used words such as 'carnage,' 'depletion,' 'disrepair' and 'sad' to describe his own country."[44] But Trump was obviously not disparaging his own country. He was accurately describing the pain and devastation that decades of "progressive" social policy had wreaked on a country he loved and wanted to repair.

In an article titled "The Meaning of 'American Carnage,'" *Slate* writer Jamelle Bouie echoed the same anti-Trump sentiments, imputing to the president even more sinister agendas: "There's a small problem with this image [of inner city carnage]. It's a fantasy. And it's a fantasy that serves a particular purpose: to demonize groups and protest movements organized around police reform." In other words, it's not blacks killing blacks on the streets of Chicago and Baltimore—it's cops killing blacks. Bouie continued: "But this isn't demonization for its own sake; it's central to the president's larger political vision, a white identity politics that looks with skepticism and hostility toward claims of racial injustice. . . . How should we understand President Trump's pledge to stop so-called American carnage? We should understand it as part and parcel of . . . white racial nationalism."[45]

A better question might be: Why did these writers twist Trump's words to mean the exact *opposite* of what he said? Were they so blinded by ideology and hate that they couldn't grasp their plain meaning? Trump was pledging to help inner-city victims of Democratic corruption and black-on-black violence. Without any evidence they turned Trump's pledge into a "white nationalist" crusade against minorities and the poor.

Before Trump, no white Republican would have dared take on Representative Cummings and the black power structure in Baltimore. It would have been political suicide. Liberal black politicians are protected from scrutiny and criticism by the politically correct dogma that "blacks can't be racist" because they allegedly have no power—a ridiculous proposition at best. As a result, the problems of America's inner cities continue to fester because black politicians are a protected species and one-party regimes are never held accountable. The Democrats have ruled—and ruined—cities like Baltimore, Washington, Chicago, and Detroit precisely because of this politically correct racism and Republican fears of being so labeled.

Why did Trump have the ability to confront this issue head on, while other Republicans did not? Because politically he was a "second-thoughter." Prior to his run for the presidency, Trump was not a partisan conservative but an influence buyer, supporting candidates from both political parties. In fact, according to National Public Radio, from 1989 to 2009, most of Trump's political donations went to Democrats.[46] He had a pro-choice position on abortion and a pro-choice position on school vouchers. In his 2000 book, *The America We Deserve*, Trump referred to his friend, the black pastor Floyd Flake, and to Flake's endorsement of school choice. Then Trump voiced his own support for the program in these words:

Nobody's more locked into underperforming public schools than poor kids and their families. And let's call this idea that poor urban parents aren't capable of making good educational choices for their children what it is: racism. These parents worry for their children as much as families in Shaker Heights or Beverly Hills—and probably more so.[47]

Democrat teacher unions have long declared war on vouchers and charter schools that might improve the educational prospects of inner-city kids. They prefer public school failure, which has been proceeding without interruption for the last fifty and more years, to a public school success that would weaken their power and benefit black children.

In other words, long before Trump became president he had paid his dues as a supporter of equal opportunities for all Americans of all colors and classes. Consequently, he had a clear conscience when it came to addressing issues like Baltimore, and a resulting confidence that allowed him to speak his mind even when doing so risked running afoul of PC prejudices on the racial left.

Con Man Al

As the left raged at Trump for exposing the failed governance of Elijah Cummings, Trump decided to pour gasoline on the fire: "Baltimore, under the leadership of Elijah Cummings, has the worst Crime Statistics in the Nation," Trump tweeted. "25 years of all talk, no action! So tired of listening to the same old Bull. . . . *Next, Reverend Al will show up to complain & protest.* Nothing will get done for the people in need. Sad!" [Emphasis added.]

Sharpton took the bait and called a press conference at which he fired back: "[Trump] has a particular venom for blacks and people of color. He doesn't refer to any of his other opponents or critics as 'infested.'"[48] Sharpton's slanders drew a blistering response from Trump, who had no thought of backing down: "Al is a con man, a troublemaker, always looking for a score. Just doing his thing. . . . Hates Whites & Cops!"[49]

It was classic Trump—no genuflection to political correctness, or to Sharpton's phony reputation as a "civil rights leader." Instead Trump called Sharpton out as the scoundrel he was. Conservatives immediately followed by posting a 1992 video of Sharpton, side by side with the notorious black supremacist and Jew-hater Louis Farrakhan, screaming "I believe in offing the pigs [cops]." Another video from 1994 surfaced in which Sharpton raved: "White folks was in the caves while we [blacks] was building empires. . . . We built pyramids before Donald Trump ever knew what architecture was. . . . We taught philosophy and astrology and mathematics before Socrates and them Greek homos ever got around to it."[50]

Sharpton had become a national figure in 1987 as a racial demagogue championing the false claims of a disturbed teenager named Tawana Brawley, who accused four white men including two law-enforcement officials of raping her, smearing her body with feces, and writing racial slurs on her belly. The story was soon exposed by a grand jury as a lie—Brawley invented the story to avoid being beaten by her father for staying out late. But this didn't deter Sharpton from pursuing the men Brawley had libeled, harassing them for six years as rapists and racists. Prosecutor Steven Pagones, whose life fell apart under Sharpton's malicious attacks, sued his assailant for libel. Pagones was awarded a $65,000 judgment, but Sharpton never paid the restitution or apologized.

In 1991 Sharpton incited three days of anti-Jewish riots in the Crown Heights section of Brooklyn after a seven-year-old black child named Gavin Cato was accidently run over by the motorcade of a Hasidic rabbi. In retaliation, a mob of young blacks stabbed a twenty-nine-year-old rabbinic student named Yankel Rosenbaum to death. Sharpton harangued the crowd that gathered for Gavin Cato's funeral referring to the orthodox Jewish community as "diamond merchants." Said Sharpton: "All we want to say is what Jesus said. If you offend one of these little ones, you got to pay for it. No compromise, no meetings, no *kaffe klatsch*, no skinnin' and grinnin'. Pay for your deeds." The rioting in Crown Heights lasted for three days, leaving 152 police officers and 38 civilians injured.

Sharpton followed his performance in Crown Heights with a campaign to drive the Jewish owner of Freddy's Fashion Mart out of Harlem, describing him as a "white interloper." Responding to Sharpton's call to action, one of Sharpton's followers torched the store, killing eight people including the arsonist, all of them Hispanic and black.[51]

Kissing the Reverend's Ring

Sharpton's subsequent resurrection as a "civil rights leader" came when Barack Obama anointed him as his unofficial "chief adviser" on civil rights. An illuminating view of this racial moment was provided by Professor Glenn Loury, an African American, anti-Trump Democrat. In a *New York Times* op-ed column, Loury asked, "Why Are Democrats Defending Sharpton? They handed Trump an easy win and yoked themselves to a genuine bigot."[52] Forty-eight hours later, he explained: "That's thanks to the leading Democratic candidates for president, who have rushed to Mr. Sharpton's defense, extolling his supposed virtues as a civil-rights paragon while denouncing Mr. Trump's attack as racist. . . . To read their tweets," Loury continued, "you would think Mr. Sharpton was Gandhi-esque."

Democrat senator and 2020 hopeful Elizabeth Warren had tweeted: "@TheRevAl has dedicated his life to the fight for justice for all. No amount of racist tweets from the man in the White House will erase that—and we must not let them divide us. I stand with my friend Al Sharpton in calling out these ongoing attacks on people of color." Senator Kamala Harris followed suit, lauding Sharpton as a man who has "spent his life fighting for what's right." Former Vice President Joe Biden joined the chorus, praising Sharpton as "a champion in the fight for civil rights."[53]

Every Democrat 2020 candidate for president attended the annual convention of Sharpton's National Action Network in 2019 to kiss the kingmaker's ring and deliver fulsome praise to the racial demagogue: "The problem for Democrats," observed Professor Loury, "is that Al Sharpton actually is, as Mr. Trump put it on Twitter, 'a con man.' And not just a con man: Mr. Sharpton is an ambulance-chasing, anti-Semitic, anti-white race hustler. His history of offensive statements is longer than the current American president's. And Mr. Sharpton's worst sin—his blatant incitement to violence during the Crown Heights riots of 1991—leaves no doubt that he is not a leader, as New York City Mayor Bill de Blasio described him, who has spent his years 'pushing for justice in the teachings of Dr. King.'"[54]

The Democrats' embrace of Sharpton and his racist anti-Trump rhetoric reflected a dramatic change in the civil rights movement. No longer was the movement about equality and basic human rights, as it was in Martin Luther King's day. By aligning themselves with a repellent figure like Sharpton and a corrupt black leader like Cummings, progressive Democrats had clearly shown that their goal was just political power—not justice, not fairness, not equal rights.

DePaul University professor Jason Hill is a Jamaican immigrant who is openly gay but politically conservative. Hill describes himself this way: "I'm mixed race, but I'm perceived as being black in America. And, like any person of color who has lived in America, I've experienced my fair share of racism. But I don't see America as a nation of extreme bigotry."[55]

In his book *We Have Overcome*, Hill offers a memorable insight into the paradox of progressives who defend inner-city carnage and protect corrupt black politicians. Progressives, Hill believes, are driven by liberal guilt and low self-esteem. He writes: "If the moral meaning and purpose of your existence as a far-left liberal rests on my suffering and victimization as a black person, then you will need me to suffer indefinitely in order to continue to cull some meaning and purpose from your life. If I reject your help on the grounds that I will not let you expropriate my agency on behalf of my life, that I will cultivate the virtues in my character that are needed to emancipate my life from the hell you imagine it to be, then I've annihilated your meaning here on earth. I've identified your moral sadism in the relief of my suffering and named the moral hypocrisy of your life. It was never about me all along. . . . You needed me to suffer so you could gain meaning, atonement and redemption."[56]

In other words, the progressive search for demons no matter the facts or circumstances is rooted in a need to see themselves as saviors of people so "oppressed" they are unable to lift themselves up. A corollary of this ideology, which is known as "identity politics" is that to criticize individuals who are members of an "oppressed" group, even powerful members like Elijah Cummings, is to become an accomplice to their oppression. On the other hand, to view black leaders as part of the apparatus of oppression, as Trump suggested, is simply unthinkable—*racist*.

5

Make America Safe

AT ABOUT 4:30 ON the morning of February 28, 2019, 59-year-old Bambi Larson was alone in her San Jose, California, home, asleep in bed. In the predawn gloom, twenty-four-year-old Carlos Arevalo-Carranza, an illegal immigrant with a long and violent criminal record, broke into Larson's home. Larson awoke and struggled with the attacker. He stabbed her repeatedly, then left her bleeding to death on the floor.

Larson's friend Diane Collman later appeared on Fox News and told host Laura Ingraham, "There's no reason this beautiful incredible human being should have been butchered the way that she was—in her own bed, in her own home. It's absolutely black and white. My message is 'Please President Trump, I beg of you—keep us safe.'"

That is what Donald Trump promised to do. But he has been blocked at every turn by Democrats in Congress, in city and state governments, and in the courts. There is a political rationale to this Democrat obstruction. In 2002, liberal journalist John B. Judis and liberal demographer Ruy Teixeira published an influential book, *The Emerging Democratic Majority*, forecasting increasing Democratic Party dominance in coming elections. Their argument was that as minorities increased in number and whites ceased to be the demographic majority, American elections would swing leftward.

In the nearly two decades since the publication of *The Emerging Democratic Majority*, Democratic strategists have worked to build a Democrat majority through demographic change—by, in effect, importing large numbers of future Democrat voters through illegal immigration. Pressures within the Democrat Party to greatly expand the influx prompted President Obama to revise the immigration law by executive order—something he had previously argued he could not do under the Constitution. Under the new order—the so-called "Deferred Action for Childhood Arrivals" (DACA)— 800,000 Hispanics, whose parents had brought them to the States illegally, were granted temporary but renewable amnesty. This questionable agenda, which was resisted by Republicans, made it inevitable that immigration would become a central front in the Democrats' war against Trump.

Senator Kamala Harris called the situation at the border a "human rights abuse." Senator Elizabeth Warren warned, "President Trump is taking America to a dark and ugly place. . . . This is not what America does. We do not put small children in cages."[57] To support their indictment, Democrats posted photos of migrant children behind chain link fences. But these photos turned out to have been taken during the Obama administration, and the policy was his. In short, Obama had been able to carry out the same policy without inciting the blizzard of condemnation from Democrats that Trump was now receiving.

Rampant political hypocrisy, however, was the least problematic aspect of the war on the border. Trump had promised a wall to stem the illegal flow. But under pressure from their party's left, Democrats would not work with Trump to build the wall, which they had previously supported. Consequently, under the pretense of working to provide refuge to would-be asylum seekers, the Democrats were enabling a multibillion-dollar criminal enterprise to smuggle unvetted aliens across the border.[58]

Globalist Doublespeak

Equally alarming was the presence of a globalist anti-American movement to erase the border itself. The anti-American billionaire George Soros, the most powerful funder of the Democrat Party and the radical left, had made his goal clear. "The most crucial issue of our time," he said, "is how to overcome the obstacles posed by national sovereignty to the pursuit of the common interest."[59] The radical protesters who were also part of Soros's Resistance coalition put the agenda into a slogan. At a May Day march in Washington, D.C., Antifa and other Soros-funded leftists chanted, "No Trump. No Wall. No USA at all."[60]

As the Democrats were wringing their hands over so-called "concentration camps," the crisis at the border grew more complicated. In addition to the usual flow of illegal immigrants from Mexico smuggled across the border by human traffickers, migrant caravans set off from Guatemala, Honduras, and El Salvador, also bound for America. The largest caravans were organized by an organization called Pueblo Sin Fronteras ("Village Without Borders") also funded by George Soros.

As the numbers of illegal migrants grew and conditions in the camps deteriorated, the Democrats' "Resistance" policy continued to block the administration's efforts to resolve the crisis. Democrats refused to negotiate with the White House on closing the loopholes in immigration law that encouraged the massive illegal invasion of the southern border.

In *1984*, the classic dissection of the totalitarian state, George Orwell coined the word *doublespeak* to refer to "language that deliberately obscures, disguises, distorts, or reverses the meaning of words."[61] Throughout the immigration debate, Democrats deployed doublespeak as a weapon in their war of words. They referred to people who broke the immigration laws as "undocumented immigrants," as though someone had forgotten to document them. They called opponents of illegal immigration "anti-immigrant," and "racist" because a majority of the law-breakers were nonwhite. Of course hundreds of thousands of immigrants who are nonwhite have been admitted every year by the Trump administration because they respect the immigration laws of the United States.

What is often forgotten in these conflicts is that legal immigration requires more than documentation. It requires vetting to see if potential residents have criminal backgrounds, are carrying infectious diseases, or belong to barbaric gangs like MS-13. Legal immigration also requires applicants for American citizenship to renounce allegiance to their home countries and pledge their loyalty to the United States—something open borders Democrats like Kamala Harris and Elizabeth Warren apparently don't value or understand.

Sanctuary Cities

The lack of respect for America's borders, and the immigration laws that defend them, actually began with the 9/11 attacks. To prevent more attacks, Congress passed the Patriot Act, creating the Department of Homeland Security (DHS). The Patriot Act was bipartisan legislation that was opposed by only one senator. But it was vigorously condemned by the political left. To implement their opposition, radicals at the American Civil Liberties Union (ACLU) and a handful of similar organizations launched the "Sanctuary Cities" movement in 2004. Its intention was to hamstring DHS officials in their efforts to secure America's borders and protect American citizens under the terms of the Act.[62]

To implement their sanctuary campaign, the radicals put together a resolution that was soon signed by politically sympathetic city councils controlled by Democrats across the country. The resolution directed municipal police departments to "refrain from participating in the enforcement of federal immigration laws."[63] It was a deliberate attempt to tie the hands of local and federal law enforcement agencies while the nation was under attack. The resolution also blocked municipal officials from cooperating with federal authorities in investigating political networks with the potential for launching such attacks, unless they were planning to commit a crime, or had already committed one.[64]

The idea that security agencies must remain blind to the politics of individuals and organizations dedicated to the destruction of the United States until they can be linked to a crime is of a piece with the belief that borders should be open, and there should be no preventive vetting process to weed out migrants with criminal records. Many security failures, including the Boston Marathon bombing in 2013, can be traced to this policy of hear and see no evil until it strikes. The ACLU resolution proved to be an effective tool for handcuffing America's intelligence services, and then for undermining the efforts of the Trump administration to apprehend and deport aliens who had entered the country illegally.

Within a few years more than 500 municipalities had signed the resolution and declared themselves sanctuary cities. In October 2017, nine months into the Trump presidency, California declared itself a "Sanctuary State" in a calculated rebuke to Trump's immigration policies. In the words of the *Los Angeles Times*, the California legislation "vastly limit[ed] who state and local law enforcement agencies can hold, question and transfer at the request of federal immigration authorities.[65] The Democrat-controlled states of Massachusetts, Colorado, Oregon, Illinois, and New Mexico followed suit.

The Costs of Illegal Immigration

The economic costs of the illegal movement across America's borders are astronomical. The costs of education, welfare, and medical services already provided to illegals are estimated to be over $116 billion nationally.[66] The costs of California's plan to provide illegals with health insurance have been estimated at $98 million. Yet virtually every Democrat participating in the party's 2020 presidential debate declared their support for providing illegals health care insurance at taxpayers' expense. In response, President Trump tweeted: "All Democrats just raised their hands for giving millions of illegal aliens unlimited health care. How about taking care of American citizens first!? That's the end of that race!"[67]

Crime committed by illegals was also behind rising public tensions over the issue. According to government statistics, between 2011 and 2016, noncitizens committed 21.4 percent of the nation's crimes, not counting their immigration crimes.[68] When Social Security fraud, identity theft, and forgery are included, 75 percent of illegal aliens commit felonies according to the *New York Times*.[69]

All this background served to highlight Trump's slogan "Make America Safe Again," and to provide substance to his rally claims that a vote for Democrats was a vote to promote sex trafficking, criminal gangs, and disrespect for the law.

Two Massacres

Tensions over the border issue came to a head on the morning of August 3, 2019. That day a deranged twenty-one-year-old individual named Patrick Crusius walked onto the parking lot of a Walmart store in the border city of El Paso, Texas. He opened fire with a semiautomatic rifle, killing twenty-two mainly Hispanic shoppers and wounding twenty-four others. Crusius surrendered without a struggle. According to police "he told investigators that he wanted to shoot as many Mexicans as possible."[70]

Police immediately connected Crusius to a white nationalist manifesto that appeared on the Internet hours before the shooting. The manifesto praised the white nationalist gunman who had killed fifty-two people at a mosque in Christchurch, New Zealand. Condemning both Democrats and Republicans for complicity in the "takeover of the United States government by unchecked corporations," the manifesto added that "at least with Republicans, the process of mass immigration and citizenship can be greatly reduced." It also warned that "heavy Hispanic population in Texas will make us a Democrat stronghold."

Fourteen hours later, a second deranged individual, named Connor Stephen Betts, opened fire outside a bar in Dayton Ohio, killing nine people, and injuring twenty-seven others before police shot and killed him. Among Betts's victims were his sister and her boyfriend whom he had driven to the bar. Unlike the El Paso shooter, Betts's politics were to the left. He was a registered Democrat and had posted tweets opposing Donald Trump and supporting Senator Elizabeth Warren. He had also tweeted support for the violent leftist organization Antifa and opposition to ICE, the border security organization that the left referred to as a "Gestapo." He also posted tweets of shockingly virulent hatred against women.

Neither Trump nor the Republicans caused the El Paso shooting. Neither Elizabeth Warren nor the Democrats caused the Dayton shooting. Individuals who shoot randomly into crowds killing innocent people and accomplishing nothing are out of their minds. The political venom in their tweets and manifestos is simply twisted justification for their irrational hate and mayhem. While there are mass killers who have been indoctrinated into a death-cult ideology, they are almost always members of Islamist groups like al-Qaeda or ISIS. But when strange, sad loners shoot up a bar in Dayton or a Walmart in El Paso, they merely dramatize the fact that mentally ill people with guns can do incredible harm. But that doesn't stop demagogues from exploiting human tragedy for their own political agendas.

Blame Trump

Democrats and Republicans responded in very different ways to these two tragic incidents. Republicans focused on the mental health issues and made no effort to connect Elizabeth Warren to the Dayton shooter. Similarly, Republicans had not attempted to implicate Bernie Sanders when one of his supporters attacked a congressional baseball game and shot Republican whip Steve Scalise, wounding him within an inch of his life. After Dayton, they did not draw conclusions about immigration or progressive violence, even though three weeks earlier an Antifa leftist was killed while attacking an immigrant detention center in Washington state.[71]

On the other hand, Democrats and their media allies didn't hesitate to blame the El Paso shooting on Trump. The *Washington Post* led with a headline that summed up the accusations to follow: "Trump's Anti-immigrant Rhetoric Looms Over El Paso Massacre."[72] This was, of course, a lie on its face. Trump was not anti-immigrant but, as he never tired of saying, only against *illegal* immigration. A number of the Hispanic victims of the El Paso shooter were American citizens of Mexican dissent. The shooter was indeed a white nationalist. Trump is not. On that fatal weekend, the *Post* and the *New York Times* shared eleven similar talking points designed to link Trump to the massacre.[73]

The *Post* lie was moderate compared to what followed: "I want to say with more moral clarity that Donald Trump is responsible for this," Senator Cory Booker told CNN, demonstrating that he has no moral clarity. When asked whether Trump caused the El Paso victims to be killed, Senator Kamala Harris said "Well no, of course he didn't pull the trigger, but he's certainly been tweeting out the ammunition."[74] Presidential aspirant Beto O'Rourke agreed: "[Trump] is a racist and he stokes racism in this country, and it does not offend our sensibilities, it fundamentally changes the character of this country and it leads to violence."[75] O'Rourke's example of racism was Trump's criticism of the anti-Semitic, pro-terrorist "Squad" in Congress, consisting of Representatives Omar, Tlaib, Pressley, and Cortez, because they were "women of color."

"Well, there's no question that white nationalism is condoned at the highest level of our government," 2020 aspirant Pete Buttigieg told Fox News the day after the shootings.[76] Buttigieg's assertion was made *after* Trump issued his official statement denouncing the shootings and the racism they reflected. In the statement Trump said: "These barbaric slaughters are an assault upon our communities, an attack upon our nation, and a crime against all of humanity. We are outraged and sickened by this monstrous evil, the cruelty, the hatred, the malice, the bloodshed, and the terror. Our hearts are shattered for every family whose parents, children, husbands, and wives were ripped from their arms and their lives. America weeps for the fallen. We are a loving nation, and our children are entitled to grow up in a just, peaceful, and loving society. Together, we lock arms to shoulder the grief. We ask God in heaven to ease the anguish of those who suffer, and we vow to act with urgent resolve."[77]

Without mentioning the attacks on him by Democratic leaders, Trump spoke directly to their slanders that had so distorted who he was and what he intended:

> The shooter in El Paso posted a manifesto online consumed by racist hate. In one voice, our nation must condemn racism, bigotry, and white supremacy. These sinister ideologies must be defeated. Hate has no place in America. Hatred warps the mind, ravages the heart, and devours the soul. We have asked the FBI to identify all further resources they need to investigate and disrupt hate crimes and domestic terrorism.[78]

Having expressed his commitment to defeating the "sinister ideologies" of "racism, bigotry, and white supremacy," Trump seized on the moment to extend a hand to the Democrats who had abused him, saying the nation must "act as one people" and "seek real bipartisan solutions":

We cannot allow ourselves to feel powerless. We can and will stop this evil contagion. In that task, we must honor the sacred memory of those we have lost by acting as one people. Open wounds cannot heal if we are divided. We must seek real bipartisan solutions, we have to do that in a bipartisan manner, that will truly make America safer and better for all.[79]

Despite the statesmanlike tone of Trump's message, which was a considered attempt to change the political discourse, the left made no gesture to reciprocate—except one. The *New York Times*, a prime adversary of the president, ran a story with an accurate headline: "Trump Urges Unity vs. Racism." But the Democrat left was not about to let that stand. The headline elicited a firestorm of protest on the left. Democrat congresswoman Alexandria Ocasio-Cortez accused the *Times* of aiding "white supremacy" by printing it.[80]

The *Times'* editors caved. They pulled the original headline and substituted a Democrat talking point as an alternative—"Assailing Hate But Not Guns," which actually drew on the divisions that Trump had sought to overcome. Suddenly it was not racism that caused the El Paso shootings—it was guns. Trump responded to this reversal with a characteristic tweet: "'Trump Urges Unity vs. Racism,' was the correct description in the first headline by the Failing *New York Times*, but it was quickly changed to, 'Assailing Hate But Not Guns,' after the Radical Left Democrats went absolutely CRAZY!" That's what we're up against . . ."[81]

The effort by leading Democrats to portray Trump as the instigator of the mass shooting in El Paso, and their rejection of his overture to unify the country against the ideologies of hate, led one conservative scholar to call Trump the "Jew" of American politics: "The frenzy of progressive commentary blaming Donald Trump for the recent mass shootings is just the latest hysterical outburst of hatred, one suggesting that for the left the president has become the 'Jew' among politicians: The object of a unique, fetishistic hatred and paranoia, Trump is the sinister agent of the Democrat Party's festering, bitter disappointment over the sudden halt he brought to their utopian fantasies of 'fundamentally transforming America.'"[82]

6

Impeachment by Any Means

FOUR MONTHS AFTER THE Mueller Report found no collusion between Trump and Russia, and four days after the massacres in El Paso and Dayton, House Judiciary Chairman Jerry Nadler announced that his committee was opening "formal impeachment proceedings" against the president.[83] Nadler is a leftwing Democrat who had played a crucial role during the Clinton administration in securing a presidential pardon for Weatherman terrorist Susan Rosenberg. The timing and manner of his announcement was suspicious on its face.[84]

Traditionally, formal impeachment proceedings are begun when the House of Representatives passes a resolution authorizing them. But while Democrats were united in the desire to impeach, they were divided on whether such a move would be politically advantageous with a presidential election on the horizon. The previous month, the Democrat-controlled House had rejected an impeachment resolution 332–95.

House Speaker Nancy Pelosi was opposed to impeachment proceedings. "Impeachment is so divisive to the country," she said, "that unless there's something so compelling and overwhelming and bipartisan, I don't think we should go down that path because it divides the country."[85] But this statesmanlike resolve was to last only a few weeks.

Democrats had claimed that Trump incited the El Paso tragedy. The radicals in Pelosi's caucus seized on the canard to advance their desire to impeach him. If Democrats were blaming Trump for the slaughter in Texas, how could they *not* seek to remove him?

Like most of Trump's alleged sins, his alleged transgression in regard to El Paso was purely rhetorical. But is what one political faction regards as "offensive" a cause for impeachment? Or were the Democrats merely grasping for yet another pretext to reverse the presidential election they had lost?

The Plot to Stop Trump

Impeachment was the logical goal of the Resistance. The Democrats' objection to Trump was not that he didn't play by this rule or that one. Their objection was to the man himself.

By the time of Nadler's announcement, enough facts had surfaced to make it clear that the effort to stop Trump had begun as early as July 31, 2016, five months before the election. On that date, the Federal Bureau of Investigation (FBI) launched a "counterintelligence" operation against the Republican presidential campaign, which was designed to link its candidate to the Russians. A dossier on Trump, funded by the Clinton campaign and compiled by former British intelligence agent Christopher Steele, was used by the FBI to obtain FISA warrants. The warrants allowed U.S. intelligence agencies to spy on Trump and his supporters with the goal of linking them to the Russians and swinging the election for Hillary Clinton. The anti-Trump plot was spearheaded by Central Intelligence Agency (CIA) Director John Brennan, FBI Director James Comey, and Comey's deputy, Peter Strzok.[86]

The plot failed to thwart Trump's presidential bid. But its conspirators continued trying to end his presidency before the next election. Alerted to the threat the deep state actors posed to his presidency, Trump fired their field commander, FBI Director Comey. Eight days later, Deputy Attorney General Rod Rosenstein appointed Robert Mueller as special counsel charged with investigating Russian interference in the 2016 election, alleged collusion with the Trump campaign, and possible criminal obstruction of justice.

Mueller was reportedly a registered Republican with a reputation for being steadfastly apolitical. He had been appointed to Senate-confirmed positions by four presidents, Democrat and Republican, and his appointment as Special Counsel drew praise from both sides of the aisle. Senate Minority Leader Chuck Schumer, a liberal Democrat, said, "Mueller is exactly the right kind of individual for this job." The Republican speaker of the House, Paul Ryan, agreed saying, "My priority has been to ensure thorough and independent investigations are allowed to follow the facts wherever they may lead. . . . The addition of Robert Mueller as special counsel is consistent with this goal."[87]

But Mueller had serious conflicts of interest: a close friendship with Comey—one of Trump's chief antagonists, a past business dispute with Trump, and the fact he had requested that Trump pick him to replace Comey as FBI director and been turned down. As soon as Mueller got to work on the Russia collusion probe, he appeared to be anything but "independent," "apolitical," or "nonpartisan."[88]

Mueller packed his Special Counsel staff with Clinton lawyers and donors, and proceeded to conduct his investigation in a suspiciously one-sided manner. He made no effort to examine the origins of the FBI investigation of the Trump campaign, the problematic FISA requests, the leaking of classified information by Comey, or the role that Clinton and the Democratic National Committee had played in sponsoring the anti-Trump dossier compiled by a former British spy with the help of the Russians. He seemed strangely incurious that the Steele dossier—a grab bag of improbable gossip and partisan smears—was used to secure FISA warrants, which allowed America's intelligence agencies to spy on Trump and his campaign team.

For his first two and a half years in office, President Trump was dogged by the threat posed by a hostile Mueller investigation with its ability to destroy his presidency. While Mueller issued subpoenas, the Democrats and the anti-Trump media—particularly the anchors and commentators on CNN, MSNBC, and the three networks—made round-the-clock unfounded charges that the president was "in Putin's pocket," and "on Putin's payroll," that he was "a "Russian agent" and a "traitor."[89] These accusations reached levels so bizarre that MSNBC's Lawrence O'Donnell actually claimed that Putin had authorized the Syrian dictator Assad to use chemical weapons against his own people so that Trump could launch a rocket attack on Syrian bases and in doing so cover up his "allegiance" to Putin![90]

Mueller concluded his investigation in March 2019. By then he had expended two and a half years of effort, spent 35 million dollars, issued 500 search warrants and 2,800 subpoenas, only to come to the conclusion that there was no evidence of collusion between Trump and the Russians.[91]

Sentence First—Verdict Afterward

The Democrats were stunned by Mueller's failure to turn up even a shred of evidence that Trump had colluded with Russia—yet their baseless conviction that Trump was a Russian agent and a traitor remained unshaken. In the 2018 midterms, the Democrats won a majority in the House and took control of the Judiciary Committee, chaired by Nadler, and the Intelligence Committee, chaired by Adam Schiff. Schiff's committee lost no time in accusing Trump of obstructing justice, even though the Mueller Report failed to find enough evidence to support the charge, and even though no crime had been identified for Trump to protect.

But evidence wasn't the issue. The Democrats were in pursuit of impeachment by any means, and their hearings were a search for the crime. In defiance of Mueller's clearly stated conclusions, Judiciary chairman Nadler claimed the Mueller Report presented "very substantial evidence" that President Trump was "guilty of high crimes and misdemeanors." He was therefore initiating formal impeachment proceedings.[92] In so doing, he was also reenacting a scene from Lewis Carroll's *Alice in Wonderland*—and casting himself in the role of the pompous Queen:

> "Let the jury consider their verdict," the King said, for about the twentieth time that day.
>
> "No, no!" said the Queen. "Sentence first—verdict afterwards."
>
> "Stuff and nonsense!" said Alice loudly. "The idea of having the sentence first!"
>
> "Hold your tongue!" said the Queen, turning purple.
>
> "I won't!" said Alice.
>
> "Off with her head!" the Queen shouted at the top of her voice.

Following the precedent set by his fellow Democrats, Nadler had declared the sentence first: impeachment. Now all the Democrat-controlled Intelligence Committee had to do was come up with the crime and the verdict—a supposedly "factual" basis for the sentence they were determined to impose.

Meanwhile, at the Intel Committee, Adam Schiff and his fellow Democrats took the unprecedented step of exploiting the nation's intelligence agencies to serve their own political ends. As reported by *Politico*, "Democrats plan to use the panel—and its access to the nation's most closely guarded counterintelligence secrets—to help guide a potential impeachment of President Donald Trump, according to Democratic aides."[93] It was an obvious continuation of what

President Trump and his supporters were calling the "deep state" conspiracy to remove him and reverse the results of the 2016 election.

Democrats' impatience to impeach Trump on any pretext they could find was more than obvious. Even while Mueller was conducting his inquiries, Democrat House members like Jackie Speier and U.S. Department of Justice (DOJ) conspirators like Rod Rosenstein and Andrew McCabe were plotting to remove him under the Twenty-Fifth Amendment. Adopted in 1967, the Twenty-Fifth Amendment was designed specifically for cases where the president had been "incapacitated" by a stroke or brain damage that made it impossible for him to fulfill his duties.[94]

Impeachment to Prevent Reelection

In the wake of the Mueller Report, Jerry Nadler and his fellow Democrats on the Judiciary Committee floundered, desperate to find a crime—any crime—to justify the preordained sentence. Nadler summoned Trump campaign manager Corey Lewandowski to testify about "obstruction of justice," but Lewandowski repeatedly referred the Democrats to the facts in the Mueller Report, and the Democrats left the hearing room frustrated—and empty-handed.

Nadler and his Democrat colleagues also tried to twist payoffs to stripper "Stormy" Daniels (with whom Trump allegedly had an affair) into a violation of campaign finance laws. And they tried to make a case based on the "emoluments clause" (Article I, Section 9, Clause 8 of the Constitution), claiming Trump profited in a corrupt way when foreign dignitaries patronized any of his hotels around the world.

None of these supposed "crimes" seemed impeachable to anyone but the Trump-hating pundits on CNN and MSNBC. The attempt to charge the president with obstruction of justice seemed particularly hypocritical in light of the pass the Obama administration and these same legislators gave Hillary Clinton, who had deleted over 33,000 emails and destroyed more than a dozen evidence-filled devices *after* they were subpoenaed by Congress.[95]

On five separate occasions, Representative Al Green offered resolutions to impeach Trump for being "unfit" because the president held views that were different from his. Green's resolution distorted them in this manner:

> Resolved, that Donald John Trump, President of the United States, is unfit to be President, unfit to represent the American values of decency and morality, respectability and civility, honesty and propriety, reputability and integrity, is unfit to defend the ideals that have made America great, unfit to defend liberty and justice for all as extolled in the Pledge of Allegiance, is unfit to defend the American ideal of all persons being created equal as exalted in the Declaration of Independence, is unfit to ensure domestic tranquility, promote the general welfare and to ensure the blessings of liberty to ourselves and our posterity as lauded in the preamble to the United States Constitution, is unfit to protect the government of the people, by the people, for the people as elucidated in the Gettysburg Address, and is impeached for high misdemeanors that the following Article of Impeachment be exhibited to the Senate.[96]

In other words, Green wanted to impeach Trump for alleged views he held that Green deemed un-American but the 63 million Americans who voted for Trump didn't. Shades of the late Senator McCarthy! But then, after filing his fifth resolution to impeach the president, Green revealed a more durable motive. "I'm concerned that if we don't impeach the president, he will get reelected."[97]

Sabotaging America's Commander-in-Chief

Nadler's reopening of the impeachment push was a declaration of the Democrats' intention to carry out their resistance/boycott of the Trump presidency to the bitter end—until he was removed. While Trump was being falsely accused by the Democrats and a partisan media of being a traitor and Putin's pawn, his hands were tied in dealing with Russia—a key player in the crises in Syria, Venezuela, and the Korean peninsula. Trump could not use the great leverage of the booming economy his policies had created to entice Russia to help ameliorate these situations. The Democrats' relentless attacks on the Trump presidency weakened his international influence and undermined his ability to negotiate deals for the good of all Americans. How much these partisan attacks damaged America's national interest and national security will never be fully known. But there's no doubt the damage has been deep, widespread, and long-lasting.

Restraint in leveling attacks against a sitting president in wartime was once part of the conventional wisdom of American politics. In 1947 at the start of the Cold War, the chairman of the Senate Committee on Foreign Relations gave an epoch-making speech in which he called for bipartisan unity in the face of the threats America faced. Arthur Vandenberg had been an isolationist Republican but now stepped forward to urge his fellow congressmen to stop "partisan politics at the water's edge."

The phrase "politics stops at the water's edge" went on to become an axiom of American foreign policy until 1972, when it was eroded by the presidential campaign of Democrat George McGovern, whose slogan was "America Come Home," as though America was the problem not her communist adversaries. It was further eroded over the Iraq War, when three months after hostilities were initiated and its monstrous dictator toppled, Democrats turned against the war they had just voted to authorize.[98]

Over the next four years while the Iraq war was raging, Democrats proceeded to attack the moral authority of President Bush, accusing him of deceiving them into supporting the war by lying about the intelligence used to justify it. The accusation was encapsulated in the slogan "Bush lied, people died!" But this was a Democrat fiction, designed to cover their betrayal of the war effort. It would have been impossible for Bush to deceive the Democrats as they claimed, since Democrats sat on the intelligence committees and had access to the same information the White House did.

In the pursuit of their anti-Bush vendetta, Democrats were willing to undermine the morale of the young men and women they had sent into harm's way. As a senator, John Kerry had spoken in favor of going to war in Iraq. But just months after hostilities began, while young soldiers fought block by block in terrorist strongholds like Fallujah,

Kerry—the Democrats' 2004 presidential candidate—reversed his position. Campaigning against Bush, Kerry claimed that the war in Iraq was "the wrong war in the wrong place at the wrong time."[99] How would a nineteen-year-old soldier at the front feel upon hearing those words?

Today's hyper-partisan Democrats often seem to have forgotten what loyalty to one's country is, and what the consequences of disloyalty can mean. Ironically, the Democrats' three-year sabotage of Trump's presidency succeeded in accomplishing precisely the goal Democrats claimed Putin sought by interfering with the 2016 election. Democrats divided the country, sowed chaos in government, and undermined the effectiveness of American policies at home and abroad.

Restraint in criticism doesn't mean an absence of criticism. It means refraining from calling the president a "Russian agent," like ranking member of the Intel Committee Eric Swalwell and other Democrat leaders have, when there is no evidence to back up the claim.[100]

Disloyalty by the Democrats also had the unintended consequence of putting flesh on Trump's campaign themes. The attempts to undermine his authority as commander-in-chief made his patriotic slogans—"America First" and "Make America Safe Again"—seem all the more necessary and *partisan*.

7

America the Ugly

A WEEK AFTER LEFTWING PROTESTS prompted the *New York Times* to remove its accurate headline "Trump Urges Unity vs. Racism," Executive editor Dean Baquet called a crisis meeting of his staff. The purpose of the meeting was to discuss the new direction of the *Times'* editorial policy in the wake of Mueller's exoneration of Trump. The meeting was secretly recorded and a copy of the recording leaked to *Slate* magazine.

According to the leaked transcript, Baquet conceded that for two years the *Times* had "built our newsroom" around the Trump collusion with Russia story. The story had proved to be a fiction, though Baquet didn't concede that in so many words. Instead he merely admitted they had been "caught flat-footed." It was time for a change, he said, and the change—he announced—was to build the newsroom around white racism.[101]

Trump's response to this change of direction was swift: "The Failing *New York Times*, in one of the most devastating portrayals of bad journalism in history, got caught by a leaker that they are shifting from their Phony Russian Collusion Narrative (the Mueller Report & his testimony were a total disaster), to a Racism Witch Hunt. 'Journalism' has reached a new low in the history of our Country. It is nothing more than an evil propaganda machine for the Democrat Party. The reporting is so false, biased and evil that it has now become a very sick joke . . . But the public is aware! #CROOKEDJOURNALISM"[102]

At the meeting, Baquet's announcement evoked the following comment from one of the *Times*' staffers: "Hello, I have another question about racism. I'm wondering to what extent you think that the fact of racism and white supremacy being sort of the foundation of this country should play into our reporting. Just because it feels to me like it should be a starting point, you know? Like these conversations about what is racist, what isn't racist. *I just feel like racism is in everything. It should be considered in our science reporting, in our culture reporting, in our national reporting. And so, to me, it's less about the individual instances of racism, and sort of how we're thinking about racism and white supremacy as the foundation of all of the systems in the country.*"[103] (Emphasis added.)

And that is just what the *Times*' editors proceeded to do: Indict as racist and white supremacist the most tolerant and inclusive nation in the world. The *Times*' editors seemed to be lacking in the most basic sense of irony. America had just completed an eight-year presidency led by a member of its historically most abused minority—something no other nation in the world had ever managed to achieve. The nation's popular culture was dominated by African Americans, its national pastime by Hispanics; African American politicians ruled major cities like Atlanta, Chicago, and Baltimore, along with its capital city, Washington, D.C. Its "paper of record" was headed by Dean Baquet, an African American. How could anyone in their right mind call its citizens and culture "racist" and "white supremacist"?

Rewriting History

These slanders were, in fact, less about race than about progressives' long-standing hostility toward their own country. Progressives embrace a globalist outlook in which they regard themselves as "citizens of the world," unmindful of the blood, sweat, tears, and political genius that had created their unique freedoms and privileges. Instead, progressives view slogans like Trump's "America First" as expressions of a fascistic nationalism with which they are at war.

Trump had used the despised phrase in his inaugural address, announcing, "From this day forward, it's going to be only America first. America first." This declaration sparked a leftist outcry, which drew lengthy parallels to Charles Lindbergh's Nazi-sympathizing "America First Committee." The *Atlantic Monthly* speculated that Trump's senior adviser Steve Bannon helped write the speech, and therefore "white nationalism" was its theme, even though Bannon is not a white nationalist.[104]

It soon became a staple among progressives to portray patriotism as "white nationalism" and to link Trump and his supporters to Hitlerism and the Ku Klux Klan. For example, Sarah Churchwell, author of *Behold, America*—a 2018 book that explains Trumpism in light of white nationalism and the Klan—wrote in the *Guardian* that Trump's slogan, "America First," is a dog whistle to his racist supporters:

> It was a disturbing phrase; think pieces on the slogan's history began to sprout up, explaining that it stretches back to efforts to keep the US out of the Second World War. In fact, "America first" has a much longer and darker history than that—one deeply entangled with the country's brutal legacy of slavery and white nationalism, its conflicted relationship to immigration, nativism and xenophobia. Gradually, the complex and often terrible tale this slogan represents was lost to mainstream history—but kept alive by underground fascist movements. "America first" is, to put it plainly, a dog whistle.[105]

"White nationalism," a ridiculous term applied to Trump, actually describes a now marginal community of true believers whom Trump has repeatedly condemned. Attacking "white nationalism" is a safe way Trump's enemies can express their hostility toward America and maintain their progressive values at the same time.

Baquet's new editorial direction was going to be based on what he called, "The 1619 Project." This project was previewed by *Times* editorial board member Mara Gay in the following words: "In the days and weeks to come, we will publish essays demonstrating that nearly everything that has made America exceptional grew out of slavery."[106] The project was supported by the Pulitzer Center and the National Museum of African American History. According to a senior policy fellow at the Center of the American Experiment, "The Pulitzer Center on Crisis Reporting has packaged it as a curriculum, with study guides and activities for teachers and students. College students across the country are absorbing its claims."[107]

In a formal statement, the *Times* editorial board described its project this way: "The 1619 Project is a major initiative from the *New York Times* observing the 400th anniversary of the beginning of American slavery. It aims to reframe the country's history, understanding 1619 as our true founding, and placing the consequences of slavery and the contributions of black Americans at the very center of the story we tell ourselves about who we are."[108]

These sentences consist of several historically illiterate—and racist—lies. They might be understandable if they had been put together by the psychological warfare unit of an enemy power. But assembled by the editorial board of America's premier newspaper, they were a disturbing indication of the derangement of the times.

To begin with, the term "America" is one that has applied to South, Central, and North America since 1507.[109] "American slavery" dates back thousands of years, but this is not what the *Times* editors have in mind. The "America" targeted by the *Times*' board was not conceived until 1776 or formally constituted until 1787, more than 150 years after 1619. American slavery lasted for only 76 years—not 400—until the Emancipation Proclamation. The slaves who were brought to the British colonies in 1619 were brought by people who identified as Englishmen, not "Americans." Moreover, they were enslaved by black Africans who sold them at slave auctions in Ghana and Benin. A proper "founding" for black slavery would go back several thousand years, and would not even involve white—let alone American—slave traders. The *Times'* 1619 Project is a project conceived in hate—hate for white people and hate for the nation they created, the center of whose story is America's dedication to liberty and equality.

To label 1619 as the year of America's "founding" and "the beginning of American slavery," and to call the slaves brought to the Virginia colony in that year "black Americans" is an act of repulsive defamation. It is a hateful lie based on a very pure form of racism, since the obvious continuity between the English colonies that existed in 1619 and the nation that was conceived in 1776 as a *rebellion against England and its empire* is that the majority of both populations were white. But their philosophies regarding slavery were diametrically opposed. That's why it took a Revolutionary War to resolve them.

In fact, one rarely discussed historical detail is that whites were not the only slaveholders in America. Blacks owned slaves in Louisiana, Virginia, and South Carolina as well.[110] Thousands of enslaved blacks were also owned by Cherokees and went on the "Trail of Tears" with their Native American owners during the removal to the Indian Territory in the 1830s.[111]

What the *Times'* 1619 Project seeks to erase is the fact of the American Revolution—that in 1776 a "new nation conceived in liberty and dedicated to the proposition that all men are created equal" was born. This America immediately began freeing the slaves that had come with the British Empire and, within a few generations, completed the liberation process through a civil war—the bloodiest conflict in American history—at a cost of over 600,000 lives.

The Nation That Freed the Slaves

This was a revolutionary promise realized more than half a century prior to the *Times* calumny, when the Civil Rights Acts provided full citizenship rights to blacks. Since slavery was a normal institution in all societies for 3,000 years before 1776, America should rightly be seen not as a "founder" of slavery but its grave digger.

The North American continent imported 330,000 slaves out of a world slave trade of over 50 million. America abolished the slave trade in 1808. Compared to other slave systems like Brazil where the slave population had to be replaced every year because of the brutal conditions, America's slave population increased in the years 1800 to 1865 from 400,000 to 4 million because of the milder conditions that largely prevailed in the plantation system.[112]

Slavery was abolished in America and then throughout the Western Hemisphere by the sacrifice of 350,000 mainly white Union soldiers who had never owned slaves but gave their lives to free their black brothers and sisters. Because of Americans' leading role in abolishing slavery and in articulating the principles of universal equality and freedom, America is more properly seen as a gift to black people despite the suffering they endured before the system was ended. For comparison, slavery still exists in Africa, 156 years after the

Emancipation Proclamation, and is a slavery in which the masters·are "people of color."

No information dredged up by the *Times* and their leftwing academic fabricators can alter those facts. The 1619 Project is a malicious propaganda exercise designed to shore up the racist, anti-white, anti-American prejudices of the so-called progressive left.

The Democrats' use of the terms "white supremacist," and "white nationalist" are particularly insidious slanders when directed at contemporary America and its president. Trump has done more for African Americans than any of his immediate predecessors, including Barack Obama. Apart from innuendo and demonstrably false claims, there is no basis for calling Trump either a white nationalist or a white supremacist, and none for describing this nation that way. Trump's "America First" theme and his "Make America Great Again" slogan capture the true nature of the political and cultural battle that divides America. It is a battle of American patriotism versus an anti-American globalism.

The left's virulent hatred of Trump drives thoughtful, learned people to rave like wild-eyed zealots. For example, Harvard law professor Laurence Tribe, once on a short list of Supreme Court nominees, tweeted a delusional claim that Trump was trying to "reverse the outcome of the Civil War." What did Tribe base this claim on? Merely the fact that Trump wants to change the immigration law on "anchor babies," which allows babies born on American soil to be the pretext for legalizing their families as well. Does Tribe truly believe that Trump was trying to reinstate slavery through changes in immigration law? Apparently so, according to

Tribe's bizarre tweet: "This fuxxxng [sic] racist wants to reverse the outcome of the Civil War. Over half a million lives were lost in that sacred cause. If you agree we can't let this lunatic get away with that, SAY SO!!! If you're silent, you're complicit."[113]

Ludicrous as these remarks are, they are not so far from House Speaker Nancy Pelosi's rancid claim that Trump's effort to put a citizenship question on the 2020 census is really a desire "to make America white again."[114] Perhaps Pelosi should seek counseling on the difference between citizenship and race. More likely she and her Democrat colleagues need a lesson in the meaning of citizenship versus a mere physical presence within America's borders. Trump wants immigrants who will contribute to our country, defend it, and respect its laws. Democrats, as Trump constantly reminds voters, don't appear to have the same concerns.

The Anti-American Left

Democrats have long used baseless racial accusations as a weapon in presidential elections. But Democrat attacks on *America* as a "white supremacist nation" are new and signal deep, ominous divisions in the country. When the *New York Times* embraces the calumnies of the hate-America left, the ship of state has entered uncharted waters.

Trump was hardly in office when Democrats and their media allies began tarring him and his top aides as "white nationalists." There were no facts to support the charge, only innuendo, and tortured interpretations of the word "nationalism" and of presidential rhetoric. One of the worst examples was the Charlottesville, Virginia, historical monument controversy. In that city, leftist protesters demanded the removal of "Confederate" monuments and memorials. The term "Confederate" in their usage extended even to statues of Thomas Jefferson and explorers Lewis and Clark (for being "white colonists").

This sparked a protest by conservatives who objected to the statue removals—not because they were racists, but because they didn't want to see the removal of these reminders of America's history. A "Unite the Right" rally was planned for August 11-12, 2017, to protest the removal of a statue of Robert E. Lee. Unfortunately, the rally attracted extremist groups, including neo-Confederates, neo-Nazis, and the KKK. During the rally, a white supremacist drove his car into a crowd of leftist protestors, killing a woman.

In response, Trump made a series of statements condemning the Klan, neo-Nazis, white supremacists, and racism in general. In one of those speeches, he added, "You also had some very fine people on both sides."[115] Even though he had just condemned racism in his previous breath, many Democrats and pundits condemned Trump for calling racists "fine people." This was not only absurd but dishonest. The "fine people on both sides" to whom he referred were those who wanted to remove the statues because they were reminders of slavery and those who wanted to preserve the statues because they were reminders of history. Trump never praised racists as "fine people"—he condemned them in no uncertain terms. But to the left, all is fair—even lies and slander—if it furthers their Resistance.

In the 2016 primaries, Trump defeated his Republican opponents who belittled and underestimated him. In the

2016 general election, Trump defeated Hillary Clinton, who had called him an inciter of racists, sexists, homophobes, and deplorables. Trump's enemies have still not learned the lessons of these defeats. Repetitive attacks on Trump as a white supremacist become a liability—not to Trump, but to his accusers, when voters see those hyperventilated attacks on Trump as attacks on *them* and attacks on *America*.

Another serious liability for Trump's accusers is their commitment to "identity politics," a tribal ideology that is, on its face and in its practice, racist. Identity Politics involves characterizing and judging individuals first by their race, then their gender, and finally their sexual orientation. A bald expression of the totalitarian nature of Identity Politics was provided by Congresswoman Ayanna Pressley, a member of the congressional "Squad" that includes representatives Ilhan Omar, Rashida Tlaib, and Alexandria Ocasio-Cortez.

A political director for former Secretary of State John Kerry, Pressley told a Netroots Nation convention in July 2019:

> [W]e don't need any more brown faces that don't want to be a brown voice. We don't need black faces that don't want to be a black voice. We don't need Muslims that don't want to be a Muslim voice. We don't need queers that don't want to be a queer voice. If you're worried about being marginalized and stereotyped, please don't even show up because we need you to represent that voice.[116]

In other words, in Pressley's eyes there can be only one legitimate black, or brown, or Muslim, or "queer" point of view. Could there be a more racist attitude than this? Yet these words were uttered and recorded at a major leftist gathering with no objections from the activists present, or from Democrats generally, including John Kerry who made a statement supporting her when Trump attacked these anti-American views. Kerry related her story of growing up in public housing, concluding: "That story identifies as more 'American' than any mantle this president could ever claim." This statement makes no sense except to an ideologue. Is Kerry really saying that being raised in public housing for the poor makes one more American than being raised by an immigrant builder?[117]

The tribal viewpoint Pressley expressed would have been anathema to America's founders, diametrically opposed as it was to the core American principle of *e pluribus unum*—"out of many one." In fact, the founders devised the American political system to *combat* her kind of tribalism.

As James Madison explained in *Federalist #10*: "Among the numerous advantages promised by a well-constructed Union, none deserves to be more accurately developed than its tendency to break and control the violence of faction." "Faction" was the founders' term for tribes based on shared interests and—worse—shared passions. They feared that if a faction succeeded in becoming a majority, it would crush individuals and minority parties, and sow domestic chaos. They regarded political parties as the most dangerous factions, which could lead to a tyranny of the majority.[118]

Tearing up the Constitution

This was the reason the founders rejected the idea of creating a democracy based on "one man, one vote," and opted for a "republic" instead. It was the reason they created a Senate in which every state was represented by two senators regardless of the size of its population. And it was the reason they created the Electoral College: to prevent a tyranny of the majority and to protect minorities.

On March 18, 2019, Democrat presidential aspirant Senator Elizabeth Warren declared war on the Electoral College on behalf of the principle of one person one vote: "Every vote matters, and the way we can make that happen is that we can have national voting, and that means get rid of the Electoral College."[119] Her Democratic Party colleagues were quick to applaud these anti-constitutional views.

Warren's attack on the Constitution resonated with Democrats still smarting over the fact that Clinton had won the popular vote in the 2016 election but lost the Electoral College. Most observers attributed this loss to the fact that Clinton had failed to campaign in key battleground states, which Democrats had won before. But the Democrats responded to Clinton's loss by vowing to tear up the Constitution and undo the founders' vision. The Democrats' obsession with Trump had radicalized them and turned them into the anti-America, anti-Constitution party.

Less than two weeks after Warren's attack on the Electoral College, leading Democrats in the Senate were getting ready "to introduce a resolution to abolish the institution," although it was a symbolic gesture since securing a constitutional amendment was not feasible at the time.[120] However, individual Democrat states like Colorado were taking steps to circumvent the constitutional process by putting together a coalition of states who would agree to award all their votes to whomever won the national vote. In other words, if the popular vote nationally were won by 10 votes for one party, every state in the coalition would award 100 percent of their electoral votes to that party, even if a majority of the voters in their state voted the other way.[121] So much for one person one vote.

As framed by Democrats, the public argument over the Electoral College was not an intellectual challenge to *Federalist #10* and the constitutional framework. It was an emotional appeal drawing on the passions and interests of the left, which illustrated exactly the dangers the Founders feared from political parties.

The loudest voice in the attacks belonged to "Squad" leader Alexandria Ocasio-Cortez, a particularly shallow but dedicated tribalist. Cortez dismissed the Electoral College as "a racist scam." Therefore, enough said. According to Cortez, "The Electoral College has a racial injustice breakdown. . . . Due to severe racial disparities in certain states, the Electoral College effectively weighs white voters over voters of color, as opposed to a 'one person, one vote' system where all our votes are counted equally."[122]

Of course, the Electoral College is not about white votes and nonwhite votes. Cortez's tribal system only includes "people of color" who are allegedly "oppressed," and their oppressors who are only white. Italians would not qualify as "of color" to Identity Politics zealots and would not therefore be on the Cortez radar. Neither would those minorities who vote Republican, or those whites who call themselves pro-gressives—all of whom are on the voting rolls in battleground states. And, of course, if blacks did not vote as a racial bloc, many states with large black populations would become part of the battleground.

The "racist scam" charge is Cortez's own brand of racism—anti-white racism. It underscores the threat posed to the American system by a Democratic Party driven by identity politics and racial tribalism.

8

The Terror Caucus

I N THE 2018 MIDTERM elections, Democrats gained forty-one seats and took majority control of the House. Among the new seats, four went to a group of radicals calling themselves the "Squad." These four far-left congresswomen immediately established themselves as the most aggressive, combative, and media-genic members of the Democratic conference. Two of the Squad members were outspoken pro-*jihadist* Muslims, one from Michigan, one from Minnesota, although all of them shared the same allegiances.

Palestinian-American Rashida Tlaib won Michigan's thirteenth congressional district seat, running unopposed in the general election. Somalia-born Ilhan Omar ran on the Democrat–Farmer–Labor ticket to become the congresswoman for Minnesota's 5th congressional district, representing all of Minneapolis and some of its suburbs.

When Rashida Tlaib and Ilhan Omar speak, they do not express the values of America's Jeffersonian democracy, or the principles of the Declaration of Independence. Though Tlaib and Omar have sworn to "support and defend the Constitution," it is clear that they are committed to tribal identity politics and a globalist rather than a national agenda. More ominously, their manifest allegiance is to terrorist forces and Islamist ideologies that are at war with America.

Palestinian Militant

Rashida Tlaib, an American-born Muslim of Palestinian-born immigrants, chose to wear a traditional Palestinian thobe—a long-sleeved, ankle-length garment—to her swearing-in ceremony and to take her oath on a copy of the Qur'an. Following the ceremony, Tlaib addressed a gathering of left-ist supporters, and assured them, "We're going to impeach this motherfucker!" Her obscene outburst against a sitting president provoked a chorus of criticism from both sides of the aisle. The language she had chosen was a breach of decorum conveying not only her contempt for the president and his office, but also for the seat she had just won in Congress. Equally important—it expressed her contempt for the due process that normally forms the basis of so serious a measure as the impeachment of a president.

Tlaib's transgression was so shocking it elicited rebukes from such dedicated proponents of impeachment as Judiciary chairman Jerrold Nadler. But no Democrat dared suggest that Tlaib, a member of three PC-protected classes, should be disciplined. When asked about Tlaib's remark, House Speaker Nancy Pelosi dismissed her choice of words as "a generational thing," and said, "I'm not in the censorship business." Pelosi's hands-off comments were an indication of how the Democrats' unrestrained attacks on Trump had made Tlaib's vulgarity and hatreds acceptable to their core constituencies.[123]

Tlaib's political community is located squarely on the fringe left: racist, anti-Semitic, and pro-terrorist. She has been a guest columnist for Louis Farrakhan's Nation of Islam paper, *The Final Call*, and received an award from the Council on American Islamic Relations—a front group for the terrorist organization Hamas. In 2014, Tlaib was a keynote speaker at a CAIR banquet in Los Angeles, and at CAIR fund-raising events after that. Among the prominent supporters of her congressional bid were such anti-American, Israel-hating leftists as Michael Moore, Noam Chomsky, and fellow Palestinian-American Linda Sarsour.

Tlaib has been funded by an array of Muslim Brotherhood-affiliated individuals and groups, including the Islamic Society of North America, the Muslim Students Association, the Muslim Public Affairs Council, the Muslim American Society, and the Islamic Circle of North America. In October 2015, Tlaib praised Black Lives Matter activists in Chicago for supporting "a Palestinian woman threatened with deportation." The woman was Rasmea Odeh, a Popular Front for the Liberation of Palestine terrorist who played a central role in a deadly bombing in Jerusalem that killed two students.[124]

Ilhan Omar

Tlaib's aggressive inaugural was quickly upstaged by fellow Islamist radical Ilhan Omar. Omar was born in Mogadishu, Somalia, in 1982. Her father, Nur Omar Mohamed, was a party propagandist for Siad Barre, the Marxist-Stalinist dictator who ruled Somalia from 1969–91 and murdered thousands of unarmed Somali civilians.[125] When Barre was toppled, Mohamed and his family fled the country and spent four years in a Kenyan refugee camp before migrating to America. Their entry into the United States was actually illegal, because Mohamed never revealed his communist background on his application for naturalization, violating the Immigration and Nationality Act.[126]

As a newly minted American, Omar went on the record on numerous occasions to defend terrorist organizations like Hamas. While a member of the Minneapolis City Council from 2013–15, Omar acknowledged that she was a friend of several young men who had joined al-Shabab, a Somali terror group allied with al-Qaeda. "They were happy young men," said Omar, "and then at some point, something happened. And that is what needs to be researched and studied. What is happening to make them feel disconnected from a community that has birthed them, that has nurtured them?"[127] In other words, in classic passive-aggressive fashion, Omar insinuated that it was America's fault they had become terrorists.

In 2018 Omar was elected to the U.S. Congress, and in that same year she gave an interview to Al Jazeera in which she was asked this question: "A lot of conservatives in America say that the rise in Islamophobia is a result not of hate, but of fear, and legitimate fear, they say, of quote-unquote *Jihadist* terrorism . . . What do you say to them?"

Omar replied: "I would say our country should be more fearful of white men across our country because they are actually causing most of the deaths within this country. And so if fear was the driving force of policies to keep America safe—Americans safe inside of this country—we should be profiling, monitoring, and creating policies to fight the radicalization of white men."[128]

This racist slander could hardly be more at odds with the truth. The majority of the nation's homicides are committed by "people of color"—blacks and Hispanics, whose victims are also mainly black and Hispanic.[129] But despite Omar's transparent racism and obvious sympathies for terrorists, her family's role in a bloody dictatorial regime, her links to the Council on American-Islamic Relations (CAIR), the Muslim Students Association, and other Muslim Brotherhood fronts, the freshman representative was appointed by Speaker Nancy Pelosi to the powerful Foreign Affairs Committee, where among other things she received top security clearances. What does this say about the priorities of Nancy Pelosi and the Democratic Party?

The Democrats and the Anti-Semite

During the first months of Omar's tenure in Congress, her hostile commitments were exposed over and over. For example, clearly referring to American support for Israel, she said "I want to talk about the political influence in this country that says it is okay for people to push for allegiance to a foreign country." The accusation of dual loyalty is a notorious anti-Semitic trope, which led to the massacre of Jews in the Soviet Union, Czechoslovakia, and other Communist satellites during the Cold War.

Omar's anti-Semitic outburst was greeted by outrage. She immediately compounded her problem by saying she was just being critical of lobbyists like the American Israel PAC (AIPAC). "It's all about the Benjamins" (i.e., hundred dollar bills), she explained, implying that congressional support for Israel was bought and paid for by rich Jews. This crossed a line that brought a stern reprimand from Pelosi and the Democrat leadership, mindful of the prominent roles Jews have in funding and leading the Democrat Party. However, Pelosi's condemnation was directed at Omar's comments rather than the congresswoman herself. This was a tactical move that gave Pelosi the opportunity to give Omar the unlikely benefit of the doubt, suggesting that she didn't realize the implications of what she was saying.[130]

This was also Omar's tack in defending herself: "Anti-Semitism is real and I am grateful for Jewish allies and colleagues who are educating me on the painful history of anti-Semitic tropes."[131] It was a politically predictable move. But her claim of innocence was difficult to square with her anti-Semitic political networks and alliances, including a series of secret fund-raisers she was holding for Islamic terror groups, her support for terrorists whose stated goals were the destruction of the Jewish state and the extermination of its Jews, and the fact that her comments seemed to move from one anti-Semitic smear to another.[132]

Trump, in particular, wasn't buying her story. "Her lame apology," the president tweeted, "and that's what it was; it was lame, and she didn't mean a word of it—was just not appropriate." Then he warned Pelosi not to ignore Omar's "anti-Semitic, anti-Israel and ungrateful U.S. HATE statements."[133] He recommended that Omar resign from Congress or the Foreign Affairs Committee. But her support was so widespread in the Democratic Party that Pelosi was afraid to remove her.

No matter what controversy they ignited, the four members of the Squad—Omar, Tlaib, Cortez, and Pressley—played the race card to deflect all criticism. When Omar was criticized for telling a CAIR audience in April 2019 that the 9/11 attacks were a case of "some people did something," fellow Squad member Alexandria Ocasio-Cortez accused her critics of "inciting violence against progressive women of color."[134]

As "women of color," the anti-American, pro-terrorist Squad members considered themselves immune from criticism. Not only did they play the race card against President Trump, they played it against Speaker Pelosi. In July 2019, after weeks of tension and sniping between Ocasio-Cortez and the Speaker, Pelosi agreed to meet her one-on-one.

Later, the four members of the Squad appeared on *CBS This Morning*. Rashida Tlaib told anchor Gayle King that Pelosi "has every right to sit down . . . in any moment, in any time, with any of us. She is Speaker of the House. She can ask for a meeting to sit down with us for clarification. [But Pelosi must] acknowledge the fact that we are women of color, so when you do single us out, be aware of that and what you're doing, especially because some of us are getting death threats, because some of us are being singled out in many ways because of our backgrounds, because of our experiences and so forth."[135]

Omar's anti-Semitic comments were roundly condemned by Republicans. President Trump, Vice President Pence, GOP whip Steve Scalise, and GOP chairwoman Liz Cheney called for Omar's removal from the Foreign Affairs Committee. There were no such calls among Democrats, though primary candidates Cory Booker and Kirsten Gillibrand did characterize Omar's remarks as "disturbing." Others, including Elizabeth Warren, Kamala Harris, and Bernie Sanders, actually defended her.

The Democrat leadership faced a daunting challenge. They were terrified of being accused of racism toward Omar and the other Squad members, and they feared alienating the Squad's supporters—even if those supporters were anti-Semites and terrorist sympathizers. Yet they also feared alienating liberal Jewish Democrats if they didn't rebuke Omar's anti-Semitic words.

Their solution, as Fox News reported, was this: "After several days of infighting and a near rebellion by rank-and-file Democrats," they passed a (toothless) resolution "to condemn virtually all forms of bigotry, including white supremacy, in what Republicans characterized as a cynical ploy to distract from Omar's remarks."[136] Neither Omar nor her remarks were singled out for censure, causing many Republicans to vote against the resolution.

A Genocidal War Against the Jewish State

Weeks later, Omar's colleague Tlaib sparked more outrage by announcing she supported a "one state solution" to the Middle East crisis, which meant that Israel would become an Islamic Republic, and its Jews would be at the tender mercies of religious fanatics who blew up pizza parlors, fired rockets into schoolyards, and targeted civilians for terror attacks because they were Jews. She followed her announcement with a podcast interview in which she claimed that Israel was created because of the Holocaust, and that "Palestinians" provided them a "safe haven" even though they had displaced Palestinians from their own land unjustly. These were all easily disproven lies, centerpieces of the propaganda war waged by Palestinian terrorists seeking to destroy the Jewish state.

Far from giving Jews a safe haven before the creation of Israel, as Tlaib maliciously claimed, Arabs inhabiting the Palestine Mandate perpetrated massacres of defenseless, law-abiding Jewish men, women, and children, beginning in the 1920s and 1930s. Under tutelage from the Muslim Brotherhood, which translated *Mein Kampf* into Arabic at the time, these Arabs, who later sought the destruction of the Jewish state, were open supporters of the Nazis and their genocidal agenda during the Second World War.

In 1948, when Israel was created, "Palestine" was a geographical designation like "New England." There was no country Palestine, and no people calling themselves Palestinian. The land on which Israel was created—as were Jordan, Lebanon, Syria, and Iraq—had belonged to the Turks for 400 years previously. The Turks were forced to cede the land when they lost the First World War. Turks are not Arabs, let alone Palestinians. The new Jewish state did not occupy one square inch of Arab land. American Indians have a greater claim on the United States than Arabs do on the land of Israel.

Yet the Jewish state was attacked on the day of its creation by the armies of five Arab-Muslim dictatorships whose stated goal was to "push the Jews into the sea." At the same time, one million Arabs decided to remain in the new state and become Israeli citizens. The Jews granted them more rights as Arab Israelis than the citizens of any Arab country enjoy to this day.

The invention of a Palestinian "nationality" did not occur until 1964, sixteen years after the creation of the Jewish state. Since all the Arabs of the area speak the same language and have the same culture, the invention of a Palestinian nationality was simply part of the war against the Jewish state. The war against Israel is more accurately seen as an imperialist war by Islamists to reconquer what they regard as Muslim land and to eliminate an infidel religion.

Like Ilhan Omar, Rashida Tlaib is a supporter of the Boycott, Divest and Sanctions (BDS) movement, a Hamas-inspired and orchestrated campaign to strangle the Jewish state. In an interview with ABC's Jake Tapper, Tlaib denied that BDS was an anti-Israel movement. "No," she said, "It's anti—it's criticizing the racist policies of Israel."[137] This was a typical propaganda lie spread by the terrorist network supporting BDS, since Israel is the only state in the Middle East that is not racist.

The founder of BDS, Marwan Barghouti, has explained in the clearest words possible the genocidal nature of its goals, which are not about "criticizing" Israeli policies: "We oppose a Jewish state in any part of Palestine. No Palestinian, rational Palestinian, not a sell-out Palestinian, will ever accept a Jewish state in Palestine."[138]

Propaganda Trip

Soon after proclaiming their support for the terrorist BDS movement, Omar and Tlaib announced a summer trip to the West Bank. A congressional fact-finding trip, including 72 members of the House and Senate, had already been scheduled, but Omar and Tlaib declined to join it. Their agenda was not fact-finding but political propaganda on behalf of BDS and the Hamas terrorist network. They arranged their travel through MIFTAH and its leader Hanan Ashrawi, a member of the executive committee of the terrorist PLO.

Ashrawi founded MIFTAH in 1998, an organization with a benign-sounding name in English: the Palestinian Initiative for the Promotion of Global Dialogue and Democracy. MIFTAH is, in fact, a virulently anti-Semitic terrorist propaganda group that has published the medieval blood libel that Jews use Christian blood for Passover observances. It has also published neo-Nazi tracts claiming that Jews rule America. MIFTAH celebrates Palestinian terrorists like Dalal Al Mughrabi, who infamously blew up a bus killing 38 Jewish civilians including 13 children, in what Palestinians describe as a "military operation."[139] The sponsorship of MIFTAH made clear that the purpose of the Tlaib-Omar trip was to spread the genocidal lies of the Palestinian terrorists and promote the BDS campaign to strangle the Jewish state.

Initially fearful of distressing the congressional Democrats, Israel offered to accommodate the congresswomen. But then Trump intervened. "Don't let them in," he tweeted. Trump's intervention persuaded Israel to change its mind and bar the Tlaib-Omar delegation. This provoked protests not only from Democrats, who chided the Israeli prime minister for showing "weakness" toward Trump's demands, but many Republicans as well.[140] These responses were an indication of how successful Palestinian propaganda had been in distorting the reality of Israel's fight for its existence against Islamic terrorists like Hamas, Hezbollah, and Iran's Republican Guard.

In responding to the ban, Omar showed how practiced a propagandist she was, telling *Politico*: "The decision to ban me and my colleague—the first two Muslim American women elected to Congress—is nothing less than an attempt by an ally of the United States to suppress our ability to do our jobs as elected officials."[141] Omar revealed her understanding of her job and its responsibilities by immediately demanding that the United States end its $3 billion annual military aid to its most important Middle Eastern ally—an ally surrounded by neo-Nazi Muslim dictatorships who had aimed 150,000 Iranian missiles at the tiny Jewish state.[142]

Angered by the double-talk around the whole issue, and by the failure of the Democrats to rein in Omar and Tlaib, Trump tweeted, "Any Jewish people that vote for a Democrat, I think it shows either a total lack of knowledge or great disloyalty."[143] This was immediately misrepresented by Democrats to mean disloyalty to Israel. They then gave it another twist characterizing it as Trump's own dual loyalty libel against the Jews. But since Israel's Islamic enemies in the Middle East have made it abundantly clear over many years that it is the Jews—not just the Jewish state—that are their enemies, it was clear that it was the Jews who were being betrayed by the Democrats' support for Omar and Tlaib.

The whole episode prompted Liel Leibovitz, an American immigrant from Israel and a Democrat, to write a lengthy piece in *Tablet Magazine* titled, "Ignore It at Your Peril: Just Because Trump Said It Doesn't Mean It's Not True: The Democratic Party Is Becoming Unsalvageable." Expressing his concern for "the political future of American Jews," Leibovitz offered evidence of "the unthinkable descent of the Democratic Party into being not just blind to anti-Jewish bigotry, but an engine of it. . . . [T]he Democratic Party has a very real and very deep anti-Semitism problem."[144]

Leibovitz went on to cite numerous examples: the Democrats who defended Omar and Tlaib after their anti-Semitic statements; the Democrats' cozy anti-Semitic associations with the Women's March co-chaired by pro-Hamas activist Linda Sarsour who is also a supporter of Louis Farrakhan's Jew-hating Nation of Islam; and the Democrats' media allies who whitewashed Hanan Ashrawi's anti-Semitism, calling her a "longtime peace negotiator" whose group is "dedicated to raising global awareness and knowledge of Palestinian realities."

Then there was HR 2047, a House bill introduced by Betty McCollum (D–Minnesota), condemning Israel's security policies toward underage Arabs who commit crimes and terrorist acts—a bill based in part on the ancient anti-Semitic blood libel that Jews are fond of abducting and abusing non-Jewish children. Leibovitz notes that many Democrats in Congress "abjure anti-Semitism in theory and yet astonishingly manage to 'accidentally' perpetrate it over and over."

During the affair, Trump summed up the nature of the Squad in these terms: "The Squad is a very Racist group of troublemakers who are young, inexperienced, and not very smart. They are pulling the once great Democrat Party far left, and were against humanitarian aid at the Border . . . And are now against ICE and Homeland Security. So bad for our Country!"[145]

While this was refreshingly frank in contrast to the Democrats' head-in-the sand denial of what they were supporting and to whom they were providing security clearances and undue authority in government, it was overly polite for Trump. These congresswomen were serial liars, fund-raisers for terrorists, and organizationally connected to a genocidal movement against the Jews of the Middle East, which neither youth, nor inexperience, nor stupidity could excuse.

9

Green Communism

A MONTH AFTER TAKING HER seat in the 116th Congress, bartender-turned-freshman-legislator Alexandria Ocasio-Cortez announced an initiative called "The Green New Deal." It contained the most radical, costly, power-grabbing government takeover of the economy ever proposed outside the Communist Party. Even more troubling, Cortez wasn't its author. The Green New Deal was a product of the progressive-socialist juggernaut that George Soros and his network of leftist tax-exempt institutions had been organizing for decades.[146]

When Cortez announced the Green New Deal, it already had the support of 600 organizations and more than sixty Democratic senators and legislators.[147] Despite this, Cortez's initiative was little more than a bare bones slate of ambitions. It offered no specific details for how the plan (if it could be called a plan) would be paid for.

Subsequent to the announcement, Cortez's chief of staff, Saikat Chakrabarti, made a surprisingly unguarded statement to the *Washington Post*. Chakrabarti explained that the Green New Deal was not actually about climate change, although that was its selling point. Instead, from the beginning the goal of its supporters was to impose socialism on America. "The interesting thing about the Green New Deal," he said, "is it wasn't originally a climate thing at all. Do you guys think of it as a climate thing? Because we really think of it as a how-do-you-change-the-entire-economy thing."[148]

The Green New Dealers proposed to replace America's free market economy with a centrally planned, top-down economic and social order, in which the federal government would be able to expropriate and direct what Karl Marx called "the means of production," and do so by executive diktat. This was the system that had already been tried in such catastrophically failed states as Cuba, Cambodia, North Korea, China, Venezuela, the Soviet Union, and all its satellites in Eastern Europe. Socialism is a system of shared misery based on the fatally flawed notion that an economy can be run by a centrally directed "plan" imposed on the population, without profit incentives to motivate individual productivity and innovation.

The fact that socialist command economies invariably fail, causing incalculable human misery, seemed lost on radical ideologues like Ocasio-Cortez, Bernie Sanders, and the now dominant progressives in the Democratic Party. Also lost were lessons to be learned from the totalitarian results of centralizing power in the hands of the state and stripping ordinary citizens of their freedoms.

The unveiling of the Green New Deal was a surreal moment. It revealed the reckless disregard radicals have for the lessons of the past and the practical effects of their utopian ideas. Cortez and her Green New Deal enthusiasts seemed simply oblivious to the devastation such a gargantuan top-down overhaul of an entire society by a few individuals at the top might wreak on the lives of its 330 million inhabitants.

Destroying America to Save the World

Ironically, the Green New Deal was being proposed at the very time when Americans had the most to lose. Trump's policies had successfully revived the economy, reducing unemployment to fifty-year lows while raising wages and employment rates for minorities. The Trump economy was breaking stock market records—a hundred by the end of his second year in office. It was reviving America's "lost" manufacturing industries, while making the nation energy independent and the number one energy producer in the world. Now the Green New Dealers proposed to destroy the fossil fuel industry with the stroke of an executive pen and imperil the most productive economy Americans had ever enjoyed.

Presented as a series of emergency measures to save the planet from catastrophe, the Green New Deal was a wish list of discredited remedies that had long been pushed by the socialist left. Some of them were just panaceas favored by the left that had nothing to do with the environment. They included cutting the defense budget *in half* with no explanation of how such a drastic reduction would impact national security, the defense industry, the economy, or the millions of workers it would displace. It was a reflection of leftist beliefs that American imperialism was the world's problem and that crippling America would "make the world a better place."

The Green New Deal also called for the decommissioning of every nuclear power plant, even though nuclear power accounted for 60 percent of carbon-*free* energy production, and eliminating it would have a negative effect on the environment.

Reckless experimentation with people's lives permeated the Green New Deal's utopian agendas. Typical was its proposal to eliminate the oil and gas industry with its 5.2 million jobs, and $64.5 billion in annual oil export revenues. The Green New Dealers offered no explanation of how the lost energy, lost jobs, and lost revenues would be replaced. They seemed blind to the way this would empower America's mortal enemies and rival oil producers, such as Iran, Venezuela, and Russia.[149] They seemed oblivious of the fact that dismantling America's oil and gas industry would end the nation's energy independence, leaving it vulnerable to energy blackmail. In their zeal to "save the planet" they seemed to forget the nation they were depending on to save it.

The Green New Deal proposed the elimination of all gasoline-driven automobiles and the retrofitting of "every building in the United States for state-of-the-art energy efficiency," which involved over 300 million structures. It called for "eliminat[ing] emissions from cows or air travel" (bovine flatulence being a major source of methane gas).

While many of the Green New Deal's proposals had nothing to do with climate change, they had everything to do with
imposing communist master plans on a passive populace.
One measure called for creating a single-payer health care
system that would put the federal government in charge of
the entire health care industry and eliminate individual freedom in choosing a doctor or a plan. Another measure called
for guaranteeing jobs at a living wage to everyone in the
United States, and providing "economic security for all who
are unable or *unwilling* [sic] to work."[150] In other words, the
Green New Deal would remove incentives to be productive
and work. In their place, like the left's failed welfare system, it
would provide incentives to expand the pool of dependency
and despair.

Ocasio-Cortez presented her proposal in the form of an
ultimatum with a ten-year deadline. If the goal of reducing
net CO_2 emissions to zero were not accomplished within the
decade, she warned, it would be too late to save the planet,
and life would become extinct.[151] Posing an apocalyptic
alternative like planetary death was less a matter of science
(though she and her supporters claimed it was) than an obvious attempt to force acceptance of an unworkable plan on
skeptics and doubters, and above all on individuals who valued their freedom. It was comparable to the slogans "socialism or barbarism," and "communism or fascism" that had
driven the agendas of totalitarian movements of the past.

The baseless claims and risk-filled ambitions of the Green
New Deal were so embarrassing that Cortez was forced to
take the announcement off her website the same day she
put it up. The proposals to get rid of cow flatulence and to

end air travel had become instant fodder for comedians, to the point where even Cortez recognized that she needed a relaunch—temporarily postponing both—to deflect the criticism. Despite the ridicule there were no significant defections among her supporters, who embraced the overarching fantasy. In fact, the ranks of Green New Deal supporters continued to grow.

Even if the Green New Deal's provisions had not been so impractical and dangerous, critics pointed out that its measures would do nothing to "save the planet." The United States was already a world leader in reducing carbon emissions. The Green New Deal offered no plan for compelling the world's worst polluters—notably China and India—to reduce their omissions. If, as Cortez claimed, the planet had only a decade to thwart the eco-apocalypse, the Green New Deal would not make a degree's worth of difference.[152]

Yet all the leading contenders for the Democratic Party's 2020 presidential nomination made its preposterous and destructive agendas their mission.

Grandiose Ambitions

Announced as it was by a freshman representative, the Green New Deal was also something of a political coup in the congressional hierarchy. House Speaker Nancy Pelosi was quick to make clear that if she had anything to do with it, the Democrat-controlled House was not going to pass the Cortez resolution. It was, the Speaker said, "one of several or maybe many suggestions that we receive. The green dream or whatever they call it, nobody knows what it is, but they're for it right?"[153]

Even the gesture of compromise Pelosi made to maintain party unity was a withering dismissal: "We welcome all the enthusiasm that people want to put on the table, and the Green New Deal is one of them, but we have to operate in a way that's evidence-based, current in its data."[154] Unfortunately for Pelosi's practicality, the power in the Democratic caucus had already shifted beneath her feet, and her caution went unheeded.

As proposed by Cortez, the Green New Deal was expected to cost as much as $93 trillion—and if previous government schemes were any indication, trillions upon trillions more. Despite Pelosi's opposition, and despite the absurd price tag, the Green New Deal garnered the support of ninety-two Democratic House members, twelve senators, and eleven of the twenty-four Democratic aspirants for the presidency, including all those likely to win the nomination.[155]

Notwithstanding its pie-in-the-sky promises, what the Green New Deal really provided was a CAT scan of its supporters' grandiose ambitions, along with their authoritarian attitudes toward a public whose lives their schemes would affect. It was not a plan to create a "democratic socialist" society, as its proponents and even some of its critics claimed. It was a plan to create a government-controlled command economy in the mold of the Communist states that had been America's mortal enemies during the Cold War.

"On my first day as president," Senator Elizabeth Warren pledged, "I will sign an executive order that puts a total moratorium on all new fossil fuel leases for drilling offshore and on public lands. And I will ban fracking—everywhere."[156] Only Communist dictators have had the power to impose such draconian sentences on millions of their subjects. So much for democracy and the sovereignty of the people.

The Green New Deal called for the destruction of the private health insurance industry, which serves 170 million Americans, as it called for the elimination of all private automobiles. It called for the elimination of whole industries, and for taxpayers to underwrite the laziness of people who didn't want to work. These extreme measures indicate a radical hostility toward free market economics and individual rights (not to mention individual responsibility). They reflect a classic radical contempt for the views, needs, and concerns of the public they are allegedly helping. And they reflect an arrogance that says to people, "We know what's best for you, and you'll agree with us, or else."

C. S. Lewis might well have had the geniuses behind the Green New Deal in mind when he wrote, "Of all tyrannies a tyranny sincerely exercised for the good of its victims may be the most oppressive. It may be better to live under robber barons than under omnipotent moral busybodies. The robber barons' cruelty may sometimes sleep, his cupidity may at some point be satiated; but those who torment us for our own good will torment us without end for they do so with the approval of their own conscience."[157]

Roadmap to a Totalitarian State

The Green New Dealers commitment to totally transform the social order by executive diktat included eliminating all internal combustion engine cars within a decade. According to the revolutionaries, the elimination of America's 267 million gasoline-powered cars was absolutely necessary to save the planet. Yet Americans have long associated private automobile ownership with individual freedom (which is why so many mass transit schemes have failed). Cars are also significant items in middle-class budgets. How would a government confiscate a quarter of a billion private automobiles without imposing a police state and inciting civil violence?

The utopians are ready with an answer. Whenever they are asked how they would implement or fund their schemes, their answer is a military mobilization similar to what America undertook in World War II. "We did it to win the Second World War, the situation we face is just as dire," according to Senator Cory Booker. In his eyes the Green New Deal is like the war against Nazism: "When the planet has been in peril in the past, who came forward to save Earth from the scourge of Nazi and totalitarian regimes?"[158]

The resolution submitted by Cortez opens with a statement explaining that to implement the Green New Deal Americans would have to live under a military regime—that is, martial law—for the ten years required to save the planet. There is no recognition by her or her supporters that during the World War II mobilization, for example, the liberal Roosevelt administration incarcerated 120,000 Japanese Americans for reasons of "national security." National security is the umbrella under which the Green New Deal's supporters view the "existential threat" from "climate change." An existential threat to the planet would justify virtually any coercive measure as a matter of security, which is why the utopians constantly invoke it.

When the Green New Deal was first announced, the Trump White House dismissed it. Administration spokesman Judd Deere told *The Hill*: "President Trump has vowed that America would never be socialist, and this administration will fight this central planning disaster," adding that it was "a road-map to destroy the American Economy."[159] Donald Trump saw the Green New Deal as an opportunity to draw a stark contrast between himself and the Democrats in the coming campaign. The progressive Democrats had boldly chosen to run on an anti-free market, freedom-crushing agenda. Trump's response was: Bring it on.

From the outset, Trump embraced his role as the anti-American radicals' nemesis. Twenty years earlier, exploring the political horizon, Trump had already identified American capitalism as the embodiment of the American dream, and laid out his political credo: "I believe in the American Dream. My business experience shows me that it works, and I want to do everything possible to see that regular Americans can enjoy the same opportunity for success and security that I have had." With these words he rallied a political constituency that progressives and Democrats had regarded as their own, and rode the support of working Americans all the way to the White House.

10

"Equality" Versus Freedom

IN THE 2016 ELECTION, 80 percent of evangelicals voted for Donald Trump. Their support was based largely on his pledge to fill a Supreme Court vacancy by nominating a justice who would adhere to the intentions of America's founders and protect religious liberty.

In many ways the divisions of the Trump era are reflections of a religious war that began in the 1960s with the banning of prayer and then religion from the public schools.[160] Virtually all the founders who created the American political order were Protestant Christians who had either fled religious persecution in Europe or were immediate descendants of those who had. The American political order is a product of their concern for religious liberty and freedom of conscience. It is an idea enshrined in the First Amendment to the Bill of Rights and is the foundation of the principle of free speech, the cornerstone of all American freedoms.

These freedoms are under assault in America as they have not been since the McCarthy Era. It is an assault waged by the progressive left who regard their political opponents as obstacles on the path to a brave new world of "social justice." Labeling opponents "racists" or "white nationalists" or "sexists" for any disagreement with their orthodoxies is the means they use to discredit and suppress what they regard as offensive speech.

Progressive Dogma Versus Heretical Facts

Dr. Allan Josephson is the former chief of the University of Louisville's Division of Child and Adolescent Psychiatry and Psychology. In 2017 he presented his views on treating children who experience gender dysphoria at a Heritage Foundation event. He had previously expressed the same views as an expert witness in court cases.

In his speech Dr. Josephson challenged transgender orthodoxy—a progressive dogma. He said the "notion that gender identity should trump chromosomes, hormones, internal reproductive organs, external genitalia, and secondary sex characteristics when classifying individuals is counter to medical science." He further said that, "transgender ideology neglects the child's need for developing coping and problem-solving skills necessary to meet developmental challenges." He concluded by advising parents to listen to their children empathetically, and then "use their collective wisdom in guiding their child to align with his or her biolog-ical sex."[161]

Several university faculty and staff members were offended by his medical views. They demanded that the university take disciplinary action against him. Acceding to the pressure, uni-versity officials removed him from his position as chief of the Division of Child and Adolescent Psychiatry and Psychology and demoted him to the level of a junior faculty member. His salary and retirement benefits were also reduced. Meanwhile his outraged colleagues were unappeased and continued to attack and belittle him.

In February 2018, Dr. Josephson learned that the univer-sity would not renew his contract, effectively firing him. At this point he filed a lawsuit. "They took all these retaliatory actions," his lawsuit stated, "with an eye to ensuring that nei-ther he nor anyone else dares to express viewpoints they find objectionable on medical and psychiatric issues."

This was an ominous episode in an ongoing modern-day witch hunt, whose effect is to overthrow the standards and procedures that have created modern medicine and academic disciplines. The witch-hunters would replace scientific meth-ods with dogma and an ideologically driven outrage that seeks not to refute the opinions it finds problematic but to destroy the individuals who express them, in effect burning the heretics at the stake.

An Act of Suppression

In 2018 the Democrat Party embraced the views of Dr. Josephson's persecutors and attempted to make them the law of the land.[162] As one of their first legislative achievements after winning a majority in the House during the midterms, Democrats passed HR 5, the Equality Act. Under the guise of extending the protections of the Civil Rights Act to the LGBTQ community, the Equality Act made the witch-hunting of heretics like Dr. Josephson a requirement of the law.

Like many pieces of legislation, the Equality Act is deceptively named in order to make it harder to oppose. Who wants to be the legislator who voted against equality? The Equality Act, which is backed by more than 500 state, local, and national organizations, attempts to give progressive dogma the force of a federal statute. Under the guise of extending the protections of the Civil Rights Act to the LGBTQ community, HR 5 was introduced in the House in March 2019, and was passed by the full House on May 17 with 236 votes (including 8 Republicans) *for* and 173 against (all Republicans). The bill was introduced in the Senate the same day as the House bill, but it was not put to a vote by the Republican leader.

In August 2019, White House spokesman Judd Deere issued this statement: "The Trump Administration absolutely opposes discrimination of any kind and supports the equal treatment of all; however, the House-passed bill in its current form is filled with poison pills that threaten to undermine parental and conscience rights."[163]

In opposing the Equality Act, the Heritage Foundation pointed out that its supporters were being deceptive in claiming they were merely extending the protections of the Civil Rights Act to other "oppressed" groups:

Where the original Civil Rights Act of 1964 furthered equality by ensuring that African Americans had equal access to public accommodations and material goods, the Equality Act would further *inequality* by penalizing everyday Americans for their beliefs about marriage and biological sex.[164]

Heritage pointed out that "similar sexual orientation and gender identity laws at the state and local level have already been used in this way. . . . Catholic hospitals in California and New Jersey have been sued for declining to perform hysterectomies on otherwise healthy women who want to become males. A third Catholic hospital in Washington settled out of court when the ACLU sued them for declining to perform a double mastectomy on a gender dysphoric sixteen-year-old girl."

The Heritage statement concluded: "This bill would politicize medicine by forcing doctors, nurses, and other medical professionals to offer drastic procedures—not in view of new scientific discoveries, but by ideological fiat."[165]

The Equality Act would also wipe out women's sports, and the many special accommodations for women that have been won through years of effort by the feminist movement.[166] By outlawing gender-specific accommodations like bathrooms, the Democrats' act would also render women more vulnerable to sexual assault.

Insensitivity to the serious negative consequences of this latest leftwing offensive reflected the failure of the self-righteous to recognize the damages inflicted by their policies. It also demonstrated a basic disrespect for—and willingness to prosecute—anyone who disagreed with them. The LGBTQ movement claims to be a defender of the vulnerable. Yet in recent decades the movement has mounted a vigilante effort to persecute religious individuals who disagree with its agendas but who have done no one any harm.

The Gender Agenda Versus the First Amendment

In 2012, a gay couple walked into the Masterpiece Cakeshop in Colorado, in a deliberate attempt to provoke a confrontation. The owner was a soft-spoken individual named Jack Phillips. The gay couple demanded he bake them a wedding cake celebrating their gay marriage. Phillips told them he would bake them any cake in the store but not a wedding cake with a pro-gay marriage slogan because it would send a message that went against his religious principles. He could not go against his religious conscience to make them that particular cake, he said, any more than he would make them a Halloween cake or a cake carrying an anti-American message.[167] He recommended another baker to them who would fulfill their request.

After leaving the store, the couple filed a complaint with the Colorado Civil Rights Commission claiming Phillips discriminated against gays. The Commission ruled against Phillips, with one of the commissioners saying of the freedom that underpins all American freedoms: "Freedom of religion and religion have been used to justify all kinds of discrimination throughout history, whether it be slavery, whether it be the holocaust, whether it be—I mean, we can list hundreds of situations where freedom of religion has been used to justify discrimination. And to me it is one of the most despicable pieces of rhetoric that people can use, to use their religion to hurt others."[168]

When the case against Phillips reached the Supreme Court six years later, the commissioner's outburst was deemed discriminatory itself. In a 7–2 decision, the Court ruled that the Colorado Civil Rights Commission violated Masterpiece owner Jack Phillips's rights to free exercise of his religion and speech, and reversed the Commission's decision.

During the six years between the original complaint and the Supreme Court ruling, Phillips was barred from baking wedding cakes. Because wedding cakes had made up 40 percent of his business, Phillips suffered a huge financial loss. During this time, he and his family were subjected to constant verbal attacks.

"We've had death threats," Phillips told ABC News. "We've had hundreds of phone calls and emails that were vile and vulgar and vicious." One death threat was phoned into his store while his daughter (who worked at the bakery) and his granddaughter were present. The anonymous caller said he was coming to the shop to make good on his threat. "I had to have [my daughter and granddaughter] go hide in the back," Phillips recalled. "It was a crazy situation."[169]

As soon as the Supreme Court handed down its ruling, a transgendered lawyer visited Phillips's shop and requested a "gender transition cake." When the baker declined to make one, the state Civil Rights Commission ruled that he had discriminated on the basis of gender identity. Phillips filed a lawsuit, but this time his persecutors backed off.

There have been many egregious cases in which state and local governments have violated the First Amendment rights of religious people. During the Obama administration, these lawsuits had the full backing of the White House. Not so with the Trump administration, in which Vice President Mike Pence has been an especially staunch defender of religious liberty. This has made Pence a target of extreme attacks from the LGBTQ radicals and organizations like the misnamed "Human Rights Campaign."

The website of the Human Rights Campaign features the headline "Trump's Timeline of Hate." The "hate" in question refers to Trump's failure to lend unquestioning support to the radical LGBTQ agenda. The site describes Vice President Pence as a "virulently anti-LGBTQ activist."[170] Pence's sin was to sign the Religious Freedom Restoration Act into Indiana law when he was governor of the state. The Religious Freedom Restoration Act was made federal law in 1993, with almost unanimous support from the Congress. It was signed into law by then-president Bill Clinton. The governors of 21 states have also signed it into law. But times change and the LGBTQ radicals had escalated their demands (and their intolerance).

In fact, Pence was generous, even Christian, in his attitudes toward the gay community. In 2015, when the mayor of South Bend, Indiana, Pete Buttigieg, announced he was gay and introduced his husband to the public, then Governor Pence went out of his way to praise him for the job he was doing as mayor and support him. Buttigieg reciprocated Pence's generosity by attacking him for his religious beliefs that were opposed to gay marriage. Accompanied by his husband on the presidential campaign trail, Buttigieg attacked Pence relentlessly—and by implication the Trump White House.

Washington Post political reporter Tom LoBianco investigated the progressive charge that Vice President Pence is an anti-gay hater and came to a conclusion that surprised even him. "His friends and advisers say no," LoBianco wrote. "To prove the point, the U.S. ambassador to Germany, Richard Grenell, a gay conservative Republican, said he and his partner have been warmly accepted by the Pences in person: 'Mike and Karen are great people, they're godly people, they're followers of Christ. They don't have hate in their heart for anyone. They know my partner. They have accepted us.' A White House spokesman argued that Pence was not 'anti-gay' because of a cordial meeting he had with Irish Prime Minister Leo Varadkar and his gay partner last month."[171] Those who know Pence well agree that the anti-gay charge against him is a baseless smear, which hasn't stopped Buttigieg from continuing his slanders.

President Trump himself told Fox News: "I think [gay marriage] is absolutely fine. I do. I think it's great. I think that's something that perhaps some people will have a problem with. I have no problem with it whatsoever. I think it's good."[172] Trump then agreed with his interviewer that, "Buttigieg's [presidential] campaign proves progress has been made in normalizing same-sex marriage."[173]

Trump and Pence set a high standard for religious tolerance and religious freedom. For the anti-Trump left, on the other hand, religious freedom is the freedom to hold whatever religious views you want so long as you keep them to yourself.

The First Amendment guarantees Americans the freedom to worship as they choose, to follow their consciences, to exercise their beliefs, and to speak them freely. So-called progressives seek to force all people of faith to bow before LGBTQ dogma or suffer the consequences. By contrast, Donald Trump has made crystal clear his belief in the First Amendment and the freedom it grants to all.

11

Trump Derangement

TRUMP DERANGEMENT SYNDROME—THE LEFT'S hysterical reaction to Donald Trump and his policies—has poisoned America's political discourse ever since Trump first announced his presidential bid. In an April 2017 Washington Post opinion piece, liberal CNN host Fareed Zakaria usefully defined Trump derangement as a "hatred of President Trump so intense that it impairs people's judgment."[174]

Zakaria originally didn't believe that Trump derangement syndrome existed—he thought it was nothing more than a trope concocted by Trump supporters to deflect criticism from the left. But Zakaria changed his mind after Trump's cruise missile strike against Syria's Shayrat Airbase in April 2017.

The strike punished Syria for its sarin nerve gas attack against the town of Khan Shaykhun in northern Syria. Zakaria had previously called Trump's Syria policy "incoherent" and had called Trump himself a "cancer on American democracy" whose administration was marked by "chaos and incompetence." But Zakaria openly supported Trump's missile strike. He pointed out that Trump was fulfilling a solemn pledge made by President Obama, who had said on September 27, 2013, that the Syrian regime must give up its chemical weapons "or face consequences." Obama blinked. But now Trump had delivered the consequences.

Media response to Zakaria's support for the strike was livid and irrational. Said Zakaria, "[Y]ou would have thought I had just endorsed Trump for Pope." One columnist called his support of the strike "nonsense" and a sure sign that the news media had "bent over backward" to support Trump. A TV journalist said of Zakaria, "If that guy could have sex with this cruise missile attack, I think he would do it."

Stunned by these rabid attacks from fellow liberals, Zakaria had to concede that, yes, Trump derangement syndrome is a real phenomenon, and that it clouds the reason of liberals whose views he generally respects. He concluded, "Liberals have to avoid Trump Derangement Syndrome. If Trump pursues a policy, it cannot axiomatically be wrong, evil and dangerous ... I believe that my job is to evaluate his policies impartially and explain why, in my view, they are wise or not."[175]

An Embarrassing Display

Pulitzer Prize–winning author Michiko Kakutani was for many years the chief book critic for the *New York Times,* putting her at the pinnacle of the sophisticated coastal elites who despise Donald Trump and want to see his presidency destroyed. In 2018 she published a book-length attack on Trump, *The Death of Truth: Notes on Falsehood in the Age of Trump*, which became a best-seller. *New Yorker* critic (and fellow elitist) David Grann called her book "the defining treatise of our age."[176] It could better be described as the defining example of Trump derangement syndrome.

Kakutani's book is a stark demonstration of what Trump hatred can do to an otherwise perceptive mind. Her book opens with a ludicrous comparison of the Trump presidency to Stalinist Russia and Hitler Germany. "Two of the most monstrous regimes in human history came to power in the twentieth century," she writes, "and both were predicated upon the violation and despoiling of truth, upon the knowledge that cynicism and weariness and fear can make people susceptible to the lies and false promises of leaders bent on unconditional power."[177]

Kakutani presents no evidence that Trump is a leader "bent on unconditional power." An indictment on the basis of assertion rather than evidence is all too typical of the anti-Trump *cadre*. Without any evidence that Trump seeks absolute power, all his signature traits that set liberals' teeth on edge—his belligerence, his exaggerations, his personal insults and attacks—become simply quirks of character. These quirks are sometimes politically useful and sometimes unfortunate, sometimes amusing and sometimes repellent, depending on one's point of view. But they are hardly omens of a Stalinist or Hitlerian evil.

According to Kakutani, Trump is someone who "lies so prolifically and with such velocity that the *Washington Post* calculated that he'd made 2,140 false or misleading claims during his first year in office—an average of nearly 5.9 a day. His lies—about everything from the investigations into Russian interference in the election, to his popularity and achievements, to how much TV he watches—are only the brightest blinking red light of many warnings of his assault on democratic institutions and norms. He routinely assails the press, the justice system, the intelligence agencies, the electoral system, and the civil servants who make our government tick."[178]

In Kakutani's hyperventilating view, the president's boasts about his popularity and achievements, and even how much TV he watches, are "lies" that somehow prove his Hitlerian intent. Denying the baseless accusations of the Russian collusion hoaxers falls into the category of truth-destroying falsehoods, as do criticisms of the press, the deep state, and anything else he finds fault with. Evidently, unlike the literati and the rest of America, the president is the only individual enjoined from offering his opinions about the issues of the day.

The *Post*'s list of 2,140 "lies," to which Kakutani refers, is similarly absurd and prejudiced, consisting mostly of items that are matters of political dispute or subject to different interpretations. Kakutani and the *Post* editors would have us believe that, because Trump responds directly to his critics via Twitter, attacks electoral and judicial corruption, and distrusts the CIA and FBI, he must be a threat to democracy itself. More likely, the view that some powerful American officials cannot be subjected to critical scrutiny is what constitutes the threat.

Kakutani's Trump derangement is embarrassingly obvious in her discussion of what she says is the administration's first "lie." She writes, "The administration, in fact, debuted with the White House press secretary, Sean Spicer, insisting that Trump's inaugural crowds were the 'largest audience' ever—an assertion that defied photographic evidence." This is how Kakutani interprets the exaggeration: "These sorts of lies, the journalist Masha Gessen has pointed out, are told for the same reason that Vladimir Putin lies: 'to assert power over truth itself.'"[179]

"Blasé About Truth Telling"

A less fevered view would recognize that most politicians routinely exaggerate their achievements. Moreover, on his election, Trump faced an unprecedented open revolt by the opposition party. Democrats made it clear they regarded Trump's election as illegitimate, and that they planned to resist, obstruct, and sabotage his presidency at every turn. They openly contemplated impeachment before he even entered the Oval Office. Seventy Democrat representatives boycotted his inauguration. On his first full day in office, he was confronted by the largest demonstration in American history, organized by the Soros-funded Resistance, led by anti-American leftists and featuring the slogan "Not My President." During a profane speech at the Women's March, the day after Trump's inauguration, onetime pop star Madonna infamously said, "Yes, I'm outraged. Yes, I have thought an awful lot about blowing up the White House."

Hearing constant threats from the progressives—resistance, obstruction, impeachment, and fantasies of violence—Trump decided to assert his legitimacy as the duly elected president. One of the ways he did so was to exaggerate the size of his crowd of inaugural supporters. He knew that 63 million people voted for him and that he had garnered a resounding 304 electoral college votes to Clinton's 277. Whatever prompted him to exaggerate, it was as far from a supposed desire to "assert power over truth itself," than Pluto is from planet Earth.

Without any sense of irony, Kakutani constructs the following picture of the president that 63 million Americans elected: "If a novelist had concocted a villain like Trump—a larger-than-life, over-the-top avatar of narcissism, mendacity, ignorance, prejudice, boorishness, demagoguery, and tyrannical impulses (not to mention someone who consumes as many as a dozen Diet Cokes a day)—she or he would likely be accused of extreme contrivance and implausibility."[180] Or perhaps of derangement triggered by irrational hate.

Kakutani then wonders how this ludicrous caricature could receive the support of so many Americans. Her answer: It is unlikely that he "would have gained such popular support were portions of the public not somehow blasé about truth telling."[181] Or perhaps just skeptical of "truth telling" by anti-Trumpers like Kakutani and her colleagues at the *New York Times*.

How intense is their hatred? For Kakutani, Trump is the "extreme, bizarro-world apotheosis of many of the broader, intertwined attitudes undermining truth today, from the merging of news and politics with entertainment, to the toxic polarization that's overtaken American politics, to the growing populist contempt for expertise."[182] In other words, in Kakutani's view, Trump is the alpha and omega of everything that is wrong with America's political culture, which has caused the death of truth, and laid the groundwork for a totalitarian regime like that of Hitler Germany or Stalinist Russia.

Truth and the *New York Times*

In *The Death of Truth*, Kakutani bases much of her claim that Trump has dictatorial ambitions on (in her words) "his lies, flip-flops, and bad-faith promises." In an implausible attempt to connect Trump to Russia, Kakutani compares Trump's rhetoric to that of Vladimir Lenin, claiming that Trump had adopted Leninist tactics of using "confusion and chaos as tools to rally the masses, to his simplistic (and always broken) utopian promises."[183]

You would think that an author who writes an entire book lamenting "the death of truth" would take great pains to get her facts straight. Yet she bizarrely attacks Trump in the area of his greatest strength, claiming he had made "bad-faith" and "always broken utopian promises." Such a charge is not only false but easily disproved.

According to the Pulitzer-winning PolitiFact (a left-tilting website that's clearly no admirer of Trump), President Trump has kept the following campaign promises: He promised to take no salary—*promise kept*. He promised to create a twenty-four-hour White House hotline for veterans—*promise kept*. He promised to slash federal regulations—*promise kept*. He promised to ban White House officials from ever lobbying for a foreign nation—*promise kept*. He promised to nominate a replacement for Antonin Scalia from a list of conservative, strict constructionist judges—*promise kept*.

Trump promised to keep the Guantanamo Bay Detention Center open—*promise kept*. He promised to move the U.S. Embassy from Tel Aviv to Jerusalem—*promise kept*. He promised to pull the United States out of the Paris Climate Accord—*promise kept*. He promised to persuade NATO nations to contribute more for their common defense—*promise kept*. He promised to halt emigration to America from unstable, terrorist-ridden nations—*promise kept*. And on and on, one campaign promise after another, kept by President Trump and checked off by PolitiFact.[184] This isn't the record of someone who aspires to be a dictator; it's the record of a democratic politician who keeps his word.

Instead of opening her screed with the loaded images of "two of the most monstrous regimes in human history," Kakutani would have been better advised to start with the death of truth at the *New York Times*. The *Times'* executive editor, Dean Baquet, conceded that for two years his paper "built our newsroom" around the Russia hoax. Then he announced he was going to move the founding of America from 1776 to 1619 in order to make slavery and racism rather than freedom and equality the nation's heritage and theme.[185]

A fair-minded Kakutani would have been concerned by the outrageous disregard for truth displayed by her own paper and the anti-Trump media generally. Every day, media representatives assaulted the public with false, character-damning accusations against Trump presented as reported "facts"— in particular that he was "in Vladimir Putin's pocket," "a

Russian agent" and a "traitor." In addition to being seditious claims, these lies had a greater impact on respect for the truth than anything said by Trump himself.

After the announcement of the Mueller Report findings in March 2019, the Trump-hating cable news outlets CNN and MSNBC suffered catastrophic declines in viewership. MSNBC's Rachel Maddow, who had regularly vied for first- or second-rated cable news program by pushing a Trump-Putin collusion narrative, lost nearly 500,000 total viewers overnight once the Mueller Report proved the accusation was baseless. The plummeting viewership of the anti-Trump networks indicates that the American people, held in contempt by Kakutani and her fellow elitists, do indeed value the truth. It's quite obviously the anti-Trump elitists like Kakutani and the editors of the *New York Times* who don't.

Every time the *New York Times* describes the president and his supporters as "anti-immigrant," which can be as often as several times a day, they are spreading a brazen lie. Trump has made eminently clear on many occasions that he welcomes immigrants—"but they have to come here *legally.*" Over a million immigrants of diverse races and ethnic origins do come to America legally every year to receive their citizenship on Trump's watch. In other words, every instance in which *Times* writers describe Trump as a "racist" or "white nationalist," because of his position on *illegal* immigration—which is frequently—they are trafficking in brazen falsehoods that are designed to undermine the authority of America's president and sow hatred toward him and his supporters, feeding the very syndrome—contempt for truth—that Kakutani pretends to deplore.

Abusing the Facts at the *New Yorker*

David Remnick is the editor-in-chief of the *New Yorker* and author of *Lenin's Tomb*, a memorable book on the collapse of the Soviet Empire. In other words, he is also an epitome of New York sophistication and erudition—and snobbery. Like Kakutani, therefore, he provides a usable measure of the irrational depths to which the liberal arbiters of the high culture have descended as a result of their hatred for the president.

In August 2019, Remnick published an article in the *New Yorker* called "Trump Clarification Syndrome," which usefully reminds readers that "Bush Derangement Syndrome" among progressives preceded the parallel attacks on Trump.[186] Remnick neglects, however, to mention that Bush—a moderate Republican, now in the anti-Trump camp—was also compared to Hitler by a left that preferred to keep the mass murderer Saddam Hussein in power rather than support their country's efforts to terminate his slaughterhouse regime.

Remnick is critical of Bush because of what he calls "the colossal disaster" of the war in Iraq. But he neglects to mention the Democrats' central role in the disaster by defecting from a war they had authorized—and doing so a bare three months after it began. By turning against the war they had voted for, they undermined Bush's authority, falsely accusing him of "lying" to gain their support. Their resistance helped to create the disaster Remnick deplores by effectively tying the hands of the commander-in-chief.

The Democrats' conversion from war-supporters to anti-war zealots and Bush haters was not motivated by anything that occurred on the battlefield. Their reversal took place because an anti-war sixties activist named Howard Dean was running away with the Democrat nomination in the presidential primaries, which were taking place at the same time.[187] Remnick cannot deal with this complex reality because the goal of his article is to turn the facts on their head and portray Trump as the one "deranged," rather than his hysterical saboteurs and detractors.

Remnick then provides the following "self-evident" proof of Trump's derangement for his readers:

> It is hard to know what [Trump's] defenders make of their hero after, say, these recent August days, in which Trump has, in no particular order, uttered, then repeated, an anti-Semitic slur about the "loyalty" of Jewish Democrats; expressed admiration for the "legendary" industrialist Henry Ford, who was also the publisher of "The International Jew: The World's Foremost Problem"; retweeted praise from a conspiracy-mongering radio host who said that Trump is practically "the King of Israel" and "the second coming of God"; reneged on a promise to establish background checks for gun buyers, after checking in for moral guidance with Wayne LaPierre, of the National Rifle Association; doubled down on a trade war with China that threatens to help spark a self-imposed recession; and cancelled a trip to Denmark because the Danish leadership had rebuffed his desire to buy Greenland in a manner that Trump, a stickler for etiquette, thought was "very not nice." In the midst of an extended, hallucinatory press session out on the White House lawn, with Marine One providing an ominous "Apocalypse Now" chopper roar to the scene, Trump gazed briefly at the sky and remarked, 'I am the Chosen One.'"

Reminick's grossly, often laughably distorted account of these incidents would not be so embarrassing had they issued from the mouth of Robert De Niro or Chelsea Handler, or some other vapid entertainer venting their personal frustrations on the president. The fact that the editor of the *New Yorker* offered them underscores the disturbing mentality of the anti-Trump camp.

The "anti-Semitic slur" Remnick attributes to Trump was his response to the genocidal advocacies of Democrats Tlaib and Omar in support of BDS, the terrorist-orchestrated campaign to strangle the Jewish state. Both women are on record desiring the obliteration of Israel and its replacement by an Islamic state. Both have keynoted fund-raisers for Hamas-related events. Hamas and its sponsor Iran (whom they have also defended) make no secret of their intention not only to obliterate Israel but its Jewish inhabitants as well. For Trump to say that support for the Democratic Party that refuses to condemn these women for their anti-Semitic, pro-terrorist, genocidal views—or even to remove Omar from the House Foreign Affairs Committee—is disloyal to the Jews (not just Israel) is morally appropriate and the very opposite of an anti-Semitic libel.

It is equally shocking to see Remnick join the ranks of the revisionists who abhor historical complexities, preferring to see everything in black and white. Henry Ford *was* a legendary industrialist, as Trump observed. He was also a notorious anti-Semite. So were Wagner and Kant. Should Americans avoid recognizing *their* musical and philosophical achievements in the name of political correctness too?

Retweeting praise from a talk show host who called him "the second coming of God" can only be regarded as serious by those who don't appreciate Trump's sense of humor, which seems to include all his detractors.

Remnick then confuses changing one's negotiating position on an issue as complex as gun control, which is what Trump did, with reneging on a promise. Listening to the political views of as large and bipartisan an organization as the National Rifle Association is hardly equivalent to seeking *"moral* guidance" from its leader. The assumption that it is merely highlights the self-righteousness of progressives like Remnick, who think they are morally superior to anyone who disagrees with them.

Remnick's sophomoric condemnation of Trump's trade war with China is accurate in one limited sense: yes, a trade war could conceivably yield bad consequences. But it could also yield very positive results. Remnick neglects to mention that doing nothing throughout three previous presidencies—Bush, Obama, and Clinton—had already produced terrible consequences for America. During that time, China had robbed the American people of more than two trillion dollars through a massive trade deficit, currency manipulation, intellectual property theft, and technology transfers. Trump deserves praise for his tough stance in attempting to end these losses. As a result of his bold action, the United States and China actually reached a "phase-one" interim deal—just a little over a month after Remnick's hand-wringing over the risk of a possible "self-imposed recession." Whether the trade deal eventually succeeds or not, its author hardly deserves mockery and sarcasm from a pencil-pusher like Remnick.

What about Remnick's complaint of a "hallucinatory press session" in which "Trump gazed briefly at the sky and remarked, 'I am the Chosen One'"? Trump made that remark while defending his China trade policy in front of reporters. Remnick quotes Trump out of context and capitalizes "Chosen One" to make Trump sound like an unhinged megalomaniac. In reality, Trump lucidly explained that his China policy was achieving what his predecessors had failed to even attempt. He talked about the billions that had been "ripped" out of the American economy by unfair trade and intellectual property theft, then concluded, "Somebody had to do it. I am the chosen one. Somebody had to do it. So I'm taking on China."[188]

Remnick even got it wrong about Marine One's "ominous 'Apocalypse Now' chopper roar" in the background. Watch the clip on YouTube. The only background sound you can hear is birds chirping in the trees.

And what about Trump's outrage over the Danish prime minister's snub? When Trump offered to buy Greenland from Denmark, the Danish prime minister, Mette Frederiksen, curtly responded, "Greenland is not for sale. Greenland is not Danish. Greenland is Greenlandic." She and other Danish political leaders dismissed Trump's notion as "absurd." In reality, Greenland would have been an important strategic acquisition for the United States, were it for sale. President Harry Truman understood the strategic value of Greenland in 1946, when he offered Denmark $100 million in gold for the vast island.

Trump regarded Frederiksen's undiplomatic language as calculated disrespect for an American president and the

United States, and he canceled his scheduled trip to Denmark. Most Americans would regard this as Trump standing up for his country. To Remnick it was merely evidence of the president's boorish character.

Whether Remnick was twisting Trump's pro-Israel statements into an anti-Semitic slur or finding a disordered mental state in Trump's innocent "I am the chosen one" comment, his Trump derangement syndrome was on full display. Remnick is a textbook case in harboring a hatred of Trump so all-consuming and zealous that it addles one's judgment.

"Trump's Mouth Is a Threat to This Country"

From the outset of the campaign to resist and destroy Trump, the focus of his would-be impeachers was almost exclusively on the president's rhetoric rather than deeds. How would one make an impeachment case over a booming economy, the lowest unemployment on record, the strengthening of NATO, the forthright support of Israel, and the defeat of the Islamic caliphate?

The attacks on Trump's rhetoric are enabled by relentless misrepresentation of what he actually has said. When Trump launched his presidential campaign in 2015, he announced that border security was going to be a priority for his White House. The attacks from the left swiftly followed. They said he had called Mexicans criminals and rapists, that he was an anti-Mexican racist.

But what did Trump actually say? Here are his exact words: "When Mexico sends its people, they're not sending their best. They're not sending you. They're not sending you. They're sending people that have lots of problems, and they're bringing those problems with them. They're bringing drugs. They're bringing crime. They're rapists. And some, I assume, are good people."[189]

As usual, Trump was speaking impromptu, so his phrasing was not exactly elegant or precise—but his meaning was clear to anyone who listened without an anti-Trump bias. He wasn't calling all Mexicans criminals and rapists. He was saying that the *illegal* crossings of the southern border included elements from the most problematic segment of Mexican society, not to mention the cartel smugglers who managed the influx. Some of those people, Trump acknowledged, were good people, but many were bringing crime and drugs. And there were notoriously too many rapes of the women seeking to immigrate. Being concerned about that is not racism. That's simply a set of indisputable facts. His opponents knew what he was saying, but they deliberately twisted his words to portray him as a bigot.

One of the leading voices in these distortion campaigns has been the anti-Trump CNN anchor Chris Cuomo who has summed up their creed; "The truth is the president's mouth is a threat to this country."[190] Cuomo concedes that Trump "likes to be provocative, and it messes with the media, and gets him a lot of attention." But he is not satisfied with that observation. "There's also a point at which what he is saying is inherently abnormal and a dereliction of his duty. His oath is to . . . faithfully execute the Office of the President. His oath is to preserve and protect the Constitution." According to Cuomo, "he's not doing either."

One would never guess from the gravity of this charge that Cuomo is referring to something as minor as Trump's frustrated lumping of the chief of the Federal Reserve with Chinese President Xi, as "enemies"—a rhetorical jab at two men thwarting his efforts to boost America's GDP.

Cuomo is aware that Trump's statement "is a metaphor" but proceeds to read into the metaphor signs of Trump's alleged adulation of ruthless dictators, while insulting Trump's defenders: "Puppets, like Senator Graham, say, 'Well, that's him being a street fighter.'" According to Cuomo: "[Trump] literally doesn't care that one [of the two] is an oppressive autocrat because he consistently is not bothered by despots, and can't stop talking like one himself." Evidently Cuomo thinks an American president should morally judge every foreign leader and pick fights with them. On the other hand, when Barack Obama, put $150 billion in unmarked bills in the pockets of the Iranian mullahs—dictators who chant "Death to America," and who hang gays from cranes—Cuomo looked the other way.

To those who prefer to look at what Trump actually does as a standard for judging him, Cuomo has this to say: "Now, I get why just his running his mouth this way might be excused by some of you because you got low, low expectations of politics. . . . [But] here's my argument: His foul mouth is just the stench of a real wound. . . . He doesn't just run his mouth about a fake brown menace. He pushes to put kids in cages. . . . He wants to remove a constitutional protection of birthright citizenship. How's that preserving the Constitution? He doesn't just talk about Islam being evil. He acts on it. He doesn't want them to come in. He tries to ban them. He doesn't just soft-pedal an objection to white supremacy. He refuses to call their murdering ways terrorism."

Typically, Cuomo's claims about Trump's *deeds* are every one of them malicious inventions, which won't be challenged on CNN. Trump has never run his mouth about a "brown menace." That is just the slander concocted by his enemies to characterize his efforts to defend America's immigration laws and borders. "Birthright citizenship" is not a constitutional protection, as Cuomo claims. In fact, it is specifically excluded by the 14th Amendment.[191] Trump hasn't tried to ban all Muslims. His ban applies to migrants from the same failed states and terrorist enclaves that Obama banned. Trump did destroy the barbaric Islamic state and its caliphate, but he has not gone to war with any Islamic nation that has not declared war on the United States. Finally, Trump has repeatedly denounced white supremacy, and forthrightly condemned murders committed by racists.

A serious credibility problem for the attacks by Cuomo, Kakutani, and Remnick is their failure to have held Trump's predecessor, Barack Obama, accountable for the sins they find beyond the pale in Trump. Take lies. Trump exaggerated the size of his inaugural crowd. To sell "Obamacare," a plan that encompassed one-sixth of the American economy, Obama lied over and over, telling Americans that they could keep their doctor and their plan under the new law, and that it would reduce their annual health costs by thousands of dollars. He also lied in assuring them that it would not be available to illegal aliens. He also abused his authority in a dictatorial manner, telling immigration organizations and television audiences at least twenty times that he did not have the constitutional authority to approve DACA or alter immigration laws and then did just that anyway.[192]

Obama lied about matters of war and peace, assuring Americans that "al-Qaeda is on the run" in order to support the campaign narrative for his 2012 reelection.[193] For the same political calculation, he lied to the United Nations and a world television audience claiming falsely that the Benghazi terrorist attack—which he knew to be a terrorist attack—was a spontaneous crowd reaction to an obscure anti-Muhammad video on the Internet that nobody saw. "The future must not belong to those who slander the prophet Muhammad," Obama declaimed to a global audience, as though he was an imam rather than the president of the United States.[194] Where were the deranged critics of Trump when *these* presidential transgressions were taking place?

And if they were silent on those occasions out of deference and loyalty to their elected president, where is their deference and loyalty to their commander-in-chief now?

12

Impeachment by Hearsay

WHEN THE $35 MILLION two-year Mueller investigation failed to find evidence of Trump collusion with the Russians, the White House was finally freed to go on the offensive. With a new attorney general in place, Trump was now able to pursue his accusers in the deep state by launching an investigation into how he had become the target of baseless charges that had handcuffed his presidency for two and a half years.

Under the auspices of the Departments of Justice and State, Attorney General William Barr, U.S. Attorney John Durham, and Secretary of State Mike Pompeo reached out to Britain, Italy, Australia, and Ukraine. They were seeking to learn how the Trump-Russia investigation originated, and the extent to which Democrats had colluded with foreign powers to undermine Trump and his 2016 campaign.

The Ukraine Connection

The origin of the anti-Trump investigations could be traced directly to a lawyer named Marc Elias with the firm Perkins Coie. Perkins Coie represented the Clinton campaign and the Democratic National Committee (DNC). Acting for both, Elias hired the strategic intelligence firm Fusion GPS to conduct opposition research on candidate Trump. Fusion GPS, in turn, hired the former British spy Christopher Steele to compile a dossier of allegations against the candidate.

Among the sources of the Steele dossier was Russia's Intelligence Service. Steele alleged that Trump and his campaign were actively colluding with the Russians to gain damaging information on Clinton—which, ironically, is precisely what Steele was doing against Trump. The dossier was then used by FBI Director James Comey to secure FISA warrants, which allowed the CIA and other U.S. intelligence agencies to spy on members of the Trump campaign, invasions of privacy otherwise forbidden by law.

Of all the foreign nations that the Obama White House and the Clinton campaign solicited to dig up dirt on Trump, none was more important than Ukraine, one of the most corrupt states in Europe. In 2014 a political upheaval ousted the Ukrainian president, Viktor Yanukovych, and threw the country into even greater crisis. The Obama administration stepped in with a billion-dollar loan and other financial assistance, putting Ukraine in a virtual receivership. Obama appointed Vice President Joe Biden to be the White House point man on Ukraine. The administration also sent political operatives, including lobbyist Tony Podesta who worked for Ukraine's pro-Russia party, and former Bernie Sanders campaign manager Tad Devine, to help orchestrate U.S. influence.

In an article in *The Hill* dated September 23, 2019, veteran investigative reporter and *Hill* vice-president John Goldman laid out the known facts about Ukrainian intervention in U.S. politics. The article was titled: "Let's Get Real: Democrats Were First to Enlist Ukraine in US Elections."

> Democrats repeatedly have exerted pressure on Ukraine . . . to meddle in U.S. politics and elections . . . [since] as early as January 2016, when the Obama White House unexpectedly invited Ukraine's top prosecutors to Washington to discuss fighting corruption in the country. The meeting . . . turned out to be more of a pretext for the Obama administration to pressure Ukraine's prosecutors to drop an investigation into the Burisma Holdings gas company that employed Hunter Biden and to look for new evidence in a then-dormant criminal case against eventual Trump campaign chairman Paul Manafort, a GOP lobbyist. . . .
>
> Democrats continued to tap Ukraine for Trump dirt throughout the 2016 election. . . . Nellie Ohr, the wife of senior U.S. Justice Department official Bruce Ohr, worked in 2016 as a contractor for Fusion GPS. . . . Nellie Ohr testified to Congress that some of the dirt she found on Trump during her 2016 election opposition research came from a Ukrainian parliament member. She also said that she eventually took the information to the FBI through her husband—another way Ukraine got inserted into the 2016 election.[195]

The Hill article also stated that the Democrats twice exerted pressure on Valeriy Chaly, Ukraine's then-ambassador to the United States. In March 2016, a DNC contractor pressured Chaly to locate Russian dirt on Trump and Manafort in Ukraine's intel files. The DNC contractor also pressed Chaly to have the then-president of Ukraine, Petro Poroshenko, make derogatory public statements about Manafort during an upcoming election-season visit to Washington. Chaly refused both requests as improper attempts to get Ukraine's help in influencing the election in Hillary Clinton's favor.

Given the Democrat-Russia and Democrat-Ukraine collusion that clearly took place, the hypocrisy of the Democrats' accusations against Trump is jaw-dropping. The Democrats accused Trump of the very crime they themselves had committed—colluding with Russia to influence an election (via the Steele dossier). When Attorney General Barr and U.S. Attorney John Durham vowed to uncover the origins of the false accusations against Trump, the Democrats tried to change the subject by concocting a *new* charge against the president—collusion with Ukraine.

Democrats claimed Trump had solicited Ukraine's help in digging up dirt on political rival Joe Biden to influence the 2020 election. The charge originated from a July 25, 2019, phone call Trump made to Ukrainian president Volodymyr Zelensky.

On September 24, 2019, Speaker Pelosi held a press conference to announce an "impeachment inquiry" of the president. At that point, neither she nor anyone else had seen the transcript of the phone call with Ukraine's president because Trump hadn't released it. Pelosi said:

The actions of the Trump presidency have revealed the dishonorable fact of the president's betrayal of his oath of office,
betrayal of our national security and betrayal of the integrity of our elections. Therefore, today, I am announcing the
House of Representatives is moving forward with an official
impeachment inquiry.[196]

Pelosi offered no evidence for any of these charges that
the president had committed treason. In fact, when asked by
reporters about the call transcript, she admitted, "I haven't
seen it, but the transcript is, uh, the fact is, that the president
of the United States, in breach of his constitutional responsibilities, has asked a foreign government to help his political campaign at the expense of our national security."[197] In
short, Pelosi made clear that this wasn't going to be a serious
"inquiry" at all. She had announced Trump's guilt in advance
of the evidence.

The Deep State "Whistleblower"

Pelosi's confidence in making extreme charges without cor-
roborating evidence stemmed from the fact that she was aware
of an alleged "whistleblower" report that was filed with the
inspector general on August 12, 2019, but had been revealed
only to Democrats at the time she spoke. On September 13,
eleven days before Pelosi's announcement, Adam Schiff, the
chair of the House Intelligence Committee, whom Pelosi was
about to put in charge of the inquiry, announced that the
inspector general of the Intelligence Community (ICIG) had
told him a few days earlier about the existence of an "urgent"
yet unspecified "whistleblower complaint."

Schiff was lying. In fact, he had known about the whistle-blower complaint a month earlier because the whistleblower had secretly come to him. For a month Schiff had kept this fact a secret from his Republican colleagues on the Intelligence Committee. When asked whether he or his staff had met the whistleblower, he repeatedly lied. On September 17, at a time he, and evidently Pelosi too, was familiar with the whistleblower and the contents of his complaint, Schiff told MSNBC, "We have not spoken directly with the whistleblower."[198]

The faceless accuser remained faceless, but details of his identity were gradually uncovered by investigative report-ers, notably Paul Sperry of *RealClear Investigations*. The whistleblower was a CIA analyst who was detailed to the White House during the Obama and early Trump admin-istrations, then returned to working at the CIA. Sperry dis-closed his name—Eric Ciaramella—in the belief that the public had an interest in knowing who was at the heart of yet another effort to impeach and remove a sitting president. Ciaramella's status as a "whistleblower," Sperry added, was compromised by the fact that IGIC Michael Atkinson found Ciaramella to have "an arguable political bias . . . in favor of a rival political candidate"—that is, Joe Biden.[199]

The whistleblower's allegiance to the Democrats explains why the accuser showed up on Adam Schiff's doorstep— and why Schiff repeatedly lied and kept Republicans on the Intelligence Committee in the dark. This also explains why Ciaramella hired two Democrat attorneys to represent him. One was Andrew Bakaj, who had worked for the CIA, the

Department of Defense, and the State Department, as well as Democratic senators Charles Schumer and Hillary Clinton.[200]

Ciaramella's other attorney was Mark Zaid, who had been openly fantasizing about toppling Trump ever since the inauguration. From his Twitter account, @MarkSZaidEsq, he tweeted in January 2017 that a "coup has started" and "impeachment will follow ultimately." He also tweeted in July 2017, "We will get rid of him, and this country is strong enough to survive even him." In response to the discovery of Zaid's tweets, White House communications director Tim Murtaugh told Fox News, "It was always the Democrats' plan to stage a coup and impeach President Trump and all they ever needed was the right scheme. They whiffed on Mueller so now they've settled on the perfectly fine Ukraine phone call. This proves this was orchestrated from the beginning."[201]

Worse, the whistleblower admitted to having no firsthand knowledge of the presidential call—the very facts on which the accusations were based. In short, Pelosi had launched an "impeachment inquiry" based entirely on hearsay evidence provided by a Trump hater from the deep state. This transparent attempt to frame the defendant would have been thrown out of any normal court of law—but not Pelosi's court.

Compounding the Democrats' credibility crisis was the fact that the accuser didn't meet the legal definition of a whistleblower. On September 24—the same day Pelosi announced the Democrats' "impeachment inquiry"—the intelligence community quietly uploaded new and revised whistleblower forms and guidance pages to the ICIG's website. The new forms and guidelines were deceptively backdated to August—the exact time frame in which Ciaramella had lodged his complaint.

Why is it significant that the new whistleblower forms were backdated? Prior to September 24, the forms and guidelines stated that a whistleblower had to have "firsthand knowledge" of wrongdoing—not hearsay. But Ciaramella had no firsthand knowledge of Trump's phone call to Ukraine. Ciaramella based his complaint entirely on reports from other people—anti-Trump, deep state officials in the White House, who may or may not have been on the call. The ICIG offered no explanation as to why the forms were backdated to August, but admitted changing the forms because "certain language in those forms and, more specifically, the informational materials accompanying the forms, could be read—incorrectly—as suggesting that whistleblowers must possess first-hand information."[202] The problem, however was not that the original forms might be misunderstood, but that they would be *clearly* understood as invalidating *this* whistleblower and his hearsay complaint.

The timing of the changes to the forms—and the surreptitious attempt to hide the backdating to August—is more than suspicious. It is damning. The form the whistleblower filed on August 12, 2019, had two checkboxes to describe the complainant's level of knowledge. One box read, "I have personal and/or direct knowledge of events or records involved." The other read, "Other employees have told me about events or records involved." The whistleblower had checked both boxes. One of those check marks was a lie.

Conspiracy to Convict?

Why did Schiff keep the existence of the whistleblower complaint secret for a month and repeatedly lie about it? Could it be that the Democrats were so eager to impeach the president they decided to construct an indictment based on hearsay evidence concocted by a politically motivated and hostile agent? Ciaramella had worked for John Brennan, Susan Rice, and other fervid haters of Trump and plotters against him. Ciaramella worked for Joe Biden in the White House on Ukraine matters during the 2016 election, while George Soros's operatives kept Ciaramella updated on Soros's activities in that country.[203] Surely all these facts could not be coincidental.

Perhaps the anti-Trump plotters thought they could get away with the whistleblower ruse because the contents of the actual phone call between Trump and the Ukrainian president remained secret. The contents of presidential phone calls to foreign leaders were never voluntarily released to the public. With the transcript of the call locked in a vault that only Trump could open, the plotters were confident they could make up their own narrative and not be challenged with actual facts.

But the next day, September 25, Trump released the transcript of the now infamous call, upending the Democrats' schemes. Here is a key passage from the transcript:

The President: I would like you to do us a favor though because our country has been through a lot and Ukraine knows a lot about it. I would like you to find out what happened with this whole situation with Ukraine. . . . The server, they say Ukraine has it. There are a lot of things that went on, the whole situation. I think you're surrounding yourself with some of the same people. I would like to have the Attorney General call you or your people and I would like you to get to the bottom of it. As you saw yesterday, that whole nonsense ended with a very poor performance by a man named Robert Mueller, an incompetent performance, but they say a lot of it started with Ukraine. Whatever you can do, it's very important that you do it if that's possible.[204]

It is clear from this text that Trump's purpose was to solicit President Zelensky's help in investigating Ukraine's role in the Democrats' effort to rig the *2016* election by providing the "evidence" that triggered the Mueller investigation.

Later in the conversation, there is a passage about former Vice President Joe Biden—the White House's point man in Ukraine during its intervention in the 2016 election. This portion of the call became the focus of Democrat attacks.

The President: I heard you had a prosecutor who was very good and he was shut down and that's really unfair. [This was a reference to Joe Biden's threat that Ukraine would lose a billion dollars in aid if the prosecutor investigating his son Hunter's corrupt company wasn't fired "within six hours." The firing followed.[205]] A lot of people are talking about that, the way they shut your very good prosecutor down and you had some very bad people involved. Mr. Giuliani is a highly respected man. He was the mayor of New York City, a great mayor, and I would like him to call you. I will ask him to call you along with the Attorney General. Rudy very much knows what's happening and he is a very capable guy. If you could speak to him that would be great. The former ambassador from the United States, the woman, was bad news and the people she was dealing with in the Ukraine were bad news so I just want to let you know that. The other thing, There's a lot of talk about Biden's son, that Biden stopped the prosecution and a lot of people want to find out about that so whatever you can do with the Attorney General would be great. Biden went around bragging that he stopped the prosecution so if you can look into it . . . It sounds horrible to me.

This is all Trump actually said about investigations and Vice President Biden during the phone call. There are two ways to look at his statements. According to Democrats, Trump pressured the Ukrainian president to "dig up dirt" on his political rival—a charge Intelligence Chair Adam Schiff had made many times during the Russia-collusion investigation without producing any evidence. An alternative interpretation of the same words would be that Trump was legitimately concerned about the apparent corruption of Vice President Biden, who oversaw Ukrainian affairs at a time when the Ukrainians were working with Democrats and DOJ officials to prevent Trump from becoming president.

The day after Trump released the transcript of his phone call, Schiff made a statement that proved to be one of the most bizarre episodes in the history of the chamber, and showed how far Democrats were prepared to go to frame a president.

Schiff prefaced his presentation with these words: "This is in sum and character what the president was trying to communicate with the president of Ukraine. It reads like a classic organized crime shakedown. Shorn of its rambling character and in not so many words, this is the essence of what the president communicates."

Then Schiff affected a ham-fisted mafia accent to impersonate the president and reprise Trump's words: "We've been very good to your country, very good. No other country has done as much as we have. But you know what? I don't see much reciprocity here. . . . I have a favor I want from you though. And I'm going to say this only seven times so you better listen good. I want you to make up dirt on my political opponent, understand. Lots of it. On this and on that. I'm going to put you in touch with people, not just any people, I am going to put you in touch with the attorney general of the United States, my Attorney General Bill Barr. He's got the whole weight of the American law enforcement behind him. And I'm going to put you in touch with Rudy. You're going to love him. Trust me. You know what I'm asking. And so I'm only going to say this a few more times. In a few more ways. And by the way, don't call me again. I'll call you when you've done what I asked."[206]

This was a shockingly malicious invention by Schiff. Trump had not asked for a quid pro quo, had not asked the Ukrainian president to "make up dirt on my political opponent," and had not given him an ultimatum to carry out his bidding. Schiff undoubtedly expected his summary to be picked up by the anti-Trump news media, heard by millions of Americans, and mistaken for the president's actual words.

But Schiff's performance was greeted with disbelief in many quarters, though not by Democrats and their media allies. Still, the deriders were numerous enough to convince him he needed damage control. "My summary of the president's call," he attempted to explain, "was meant to be at least in part parody. The fact that's not clear is a separate problem in and of itself. Of course, the president never said if you don't understand me, I'm going to say it seven more times. My point is that's the message that the Ukraine president was receiving in not so many words."

In other words, "I made it up, but it's true." But it wasn't.

The president's response to Schiff's "parody" was a damning tweet: "Rep. Adam Schiff illegally made up a FAKE & terrible statement, pretended it to be mine as the most important part of my call to the Ukrainian President, and read it aloud to Congress and the American people. It bore NO relationship to what I said on the call. Arrest for Treason?"[207]

Schiff never explained how he justified such a gross (and seditious) misrepresentation of the president's words in so solemn a forum as an impeachment inquiry. Yet Schiff's "parody" was in keeping with the Democrats' entire approach to the inquiry, which they ran as a Star Chamber proceeding, replete with secrecy, denial of due process, selective leaking of damaging claims, and suppression of contradictory testimony. Democrats controlled the release of information to the public and denied Republican members basic rights that had always been provided to the minority in past impeachments. As Republican committee member Mark Meadows observed grimly: "A hardened criminal has more rights than the president of the United States."

On October 8, 2019, White House counsel Pat Cipollone sent a letter to Speaker Nancy Pelosi and three House committee chairmen, stating that the Trump administration would not cooperate with the impeachment inquiry. Though the eight-page letter is worth reading in its entirety, this excerpt encapsulates the administration's argument:

> implemented your inquiry in a manner that violates fundamental fairness and constitutionally mandated due process. For example, you have denied the President the right to cross-examine witnesses, to call witnesses, to receive transcripts of testimony, to have access to evidence, to have counsel present, and many other basic rights guaranteed to all Americans. You have conducted your proceedings in secret. You have violated civil liberties and the separation of powers by threatening Executive Branch officials, claiming that you will seek to punish those who exercise fundamental constitutional rights and prerogatives. All of this violates the Constitution, the rule of law, and *every past precedent.*[208]

During a political rally in Monroe, Louisiana, the following month, Trump told the crowd, with chilling accuracy: "On their campaign to transform America, Democrats are becoming increasingly totalitarian: suppressing dissent, defaming the innocent, eliminating due process, staging show trials and trying to overthrow American democracy to impose their socialist agenda. . . . The radical left Democrats are trying to rip our nation apart."[209]

"A Legislative Coup"

The president's senior policy adviser, Stephen Miller, echoed the president with an equally damning description to Breitbart News of what was taking place: "The attempt at impeachment is best understood as a legislative coup against a democratically elected president, and the radical leftists in Congress are working arm-in-arm with the deep state saboteurs and their allies in the media in order to try to effectuate this illegal coup."[210]

According to Miller, the real whistleblower was Trump, exposing the elements of the Washington swamp that had conspired against him. The Democrats' whistleblower, on the other hand, was an agent of the deep state, which had been trying to prevent and then overthrow the Trump presidency for more than three years.

"The deep state," explained Miller, "is a collection of permanent bureaucrats enmeshed inside the federal government who can't be fired or removed . . . because of misguided civil service laws. They believe they know better than you, and your listeners, and the voters how the country ought to be run. At this moment in time, the deep state has a knife aimed at the heart of American democracy, and that's what you're seeing playing across your TV screens and newspapers' pages and online, with these so-called whistleblowers, who are, of course, in fact, angry hate-filled rage-driven bureaucrats determined to take down the President of the United States and illicitly and improperly using the Whistleblower Protection Act in order to effectuate their designs."[211]

How does the deep state advance its agenda? Miller explained that if the deep state careerists don't like the direction the president and his team are taking, "they will leak and spin and lie about the contents of your meetings. They'll take it to the *Washington Post* and the *New York Times* and to MSNBC. They'll share private documents, they'll share private emails, they'll share private correspondence, and then they'll spin and fabricate and lie to create their desired narrative to try to steer policy in the direction they want to steer it in, and the most dangerous expression of this—of course, we've seen—has been in the intelligence community, which is amassed with awesome power, awesome capabilities, and they're directing that and wielding that—in some cases—against a duly-elected President of the United States of America, which is a form of sabotage that should terrify everyday American citizens. That is now the situation we find ourselves in."[212]

Support for Miller's concerns came from an unlikely source in the person of Matt Taibbi, a veteran journalist who had written two best-selling anti-Trump books. In an article published five days after Miller's interview and titled "We're in a Permanent Coup," he warned of the threat to America's democratic order posed by the deep-state conspiracy: "The Trump presidency is the first to reveal a full-blown schism between the intelligence community and the White House. Senior figures in the CIA, NSA, FBI and other agencies made an open break from their would-be boss before Trump's inauguration, commencing a public war of leaks that has not stopped.

"My discomfort in the last few years, first with Russiagate and now with Ukrainegate and impeachment, stems from the belief that the people pushing hardest for Trump's early removal are more dangerous than Trump. Many Americans don't see this because they're not used to waking up in a country where you're not sure who the president will be by nightfall. They don't understand that this predicament is worse than having a bad president."[213]

This warning from Taibbi was echoed by another liberal critic of Trump—Harvard law professor Alan Dershowitz. In a talk show appearance on New York's AM 970 radio on Sunday, November 10, 2019, Dershowitz said, "Whether you're a Democrat or a Republican, whether you're from New York or the middle of the country, you should be frightened by efforts to try to create crimes out of nothing. . . . It reminds me of what Lavrentiy Beria, the head of the KGB, said to Stalin. He said, 'Show me the man, and I'll find you the crime,' by which he really meant, 'I'll make up the crime.' And so the Democrats are now making up crimes."

13

What the President Actually Did

MARK LEIBOVICH IS THE chief national correspondent for the *New York Times*. In 2013 he published *This Town* about the nation's capital. It became an instant number one best-seller. *This Town* exposed the political parasites who infest Washington, feeding off special interest money while claiming to work for the people. Leibovich cited the example of Quinn Gillespie & Associates, one of the most successful lobbying firms in Washington. It was founded by Republican strategist Ed Gillespie and Democratic strategist Jack Quinn. When Leibovich asked why these two politicos from opposing parties were such good friends, Quinn replied, "Ed got the joke."

What was "the joke?" According to Leibovich the joke had many levels. It was a joke on the taxpayers, who unwittingly supported the corrupt Washington system with their hard-earned tax dollars. It was on American voters who believed their elected representatives were dedicated public servants. With surprising candor, Quinn confessed that "the joke" is the deceptive notion that "everyone involved in the world in which we operate is a patriot." In recent years, the people have become increasingly aware that "the joke" is on us. We play by the rules and pay our taxes while the politicians laugh behind our backs and treat us like fools.

Enter Donald Trump.

Trump was elected because he is *not* a politician. He promised to "drain the swamp," build the wall, and make America great again. And he actually attempted to keep his promises. That's why official Washington hates and seeks to destroy him.

As Trump Senior Policy Adviser Stephen Miller observed in his interview for *Breitbart News Sunday*, the political power structure declared war on Trump "because this president dared to disrupt two-party betrayal of the American people over many decades: betrayal on trade, betrayal on China, betrayal on foreign policy, betrayal on our southern border, betrayal on our economy, decade after decade, year after year, administration after administration. This president dared to stand up to defy that betrayal, . . . to end that betrayal. But the people who profited like parasites off that betrayal are now the ones trying to prevent him from executing the agenda that the American people installed him to execute."

Trade and China

Trump's actions in the Oval Office did indeed reflect the priorities Miller listed. During the previous thirty years the White House—whether Democrat or Republican—had allowed foreign trading partners like China, Mexico, Japan, and the European Union to take trillions of dollars out of American pockets without any real attempt to defend America's interests by fighting for fair and balanced trade deals. In Trump's view his predecessors had shirked their presidential duty to their country and allowed America to be treated as a global "piggy bank."

Trump dedicated his presidency to redressing the injustice and securing better terms of trade for his country. In his first weeks in office, Trump signed an executive order terminating the Trans-Pacific Partnership (TPP). Pulling the United States out of the TPP was a major Trump campaign issue. At an Ohio campaign rally, he had declared that the TPP was "another disaster done and pushed by special interests who want to rape our country."

Responding to China's multibillion-dollar thefts of American technology and intellectual property, he imposed crippling tariffs to force the Chinese to agree to better, fairer terms of trade. His use of tariffs to defend America's interests were vociferously opposed as "too risky" by Wall Street, and by Democrats and Republicans alike. Despite the doubters, the Trump tariffs brought tens of billions of dollars flowing into the American Treasury. According to the *Wall Street Journal* (June 16, 2019), Trump's tariffs caused serious damage to China's economy and persuaded the Chinese to reconsider their position on trade.

On October 11, 2019, Trump announced he had finalized phase one of a trade deal with China, made possible by his "trade war" strategy. The deal covered intellectual property protection, financial services, and China's agreement to purchase between 40 and 50 billion dollars in agricultural products from American farmers. According to *Business Insider* (October 23, 2019), this was one and a half to two times the amount of agricultural products China had purchased from the United States at the highest point of U.S.-China trade relations before. The deal was still subject to the whims of an absolute and hostile dictator. But it made clear the direction in which Trump was moving and the will and energy he had put behind it.

Trump also moved to check China's military expansionism and aggressive ambitions. In April 2018, Reuters reported that the Trump administration had given U.S. manufacturers permission to share submarine technology with Taiwan. And in June of that year, *The Hill* reported the United States had opened a new de facto embassy in Taiwan as a sign of strengthened relations with that country and resistance to Chinese imperialism. In September 2018, Trump approved a $330 million sale of arms to Taiwan.

Trump's tough posture toward China led to important changes in China's aggressive policy in Southeast Asia: "Under the Obama administration, Chinese forces regularly harassed U.S. vessels navigating the South China Sea," observed the *National Interest* in September 2018. "That doesn't happen under the Trump administration."

Strengthening America's Defenses and Alliances

While eight years of the Obama administration had witnessed a steady degradation of America's military, Trump signed budgets allocating $700 billion in military funding for FY 2018 and $716 billion for FY 2019, the largest sums in U.S. history. He ordered a "Nuclear Posture Review" to ensure that America's nuclear forces would remain unrivaled. Trump released America's first fully articulated cyber strategy in 15 years, and he enacted the launch of a Space Force as a new branch of the U.S. military.[214]

In May 2017, Trump challenged European leaders to contribute more to NATO, by meeting the obligation to devote 2 percent of their budgets for the common defense. This was part of his effort to reverse the policies of past administrations, who were comfortable with American taxpayers funding the defense of rich nations like Germany that could well afford to defend themselves. Trump continued his calls for NATO countries to step up their contributions throughout 2017 and 2018. He was roundly criticized for this by Democrats who accused him of being an isolationist and attempting to wreck America's most important alliance, which had kept the peace since the end of World War II.

However, Trump's pressure had dramatic results both for strengthening NATO and relieving the United States of this financial burden. Of the twenty-seven NATO countries other than the United States, twenty-six increased their NATO defense spending (in real currency) between 2017 and 2019, adding $100 billion to the defense of the West.[215]

President Obama had built his foreign policy around lifting sanctions on Iran and bringing the terrorist state back into the community of nations, without any reform of its regime. To accomplish this treacherous goal, he turned a blind eye to the Iranian *mullahs'* chants of "Death to America" and their active support for terror, including their provision of IEDs to Iraqi militants to blow up American soldiers. He also ignored the 150,000 rockets Iran had provided to its terrorist proxy, Hezbollah, to aim at Israel. Ignoring these deeds and threats, Obama signed a deal that gave Iran a path to nuclear weapons, and he did so without adequate inspection provisions to see that the America-hating *mullahs* adhered to the already bad terms of the agreement.

Obama knew he could never sell Republican senators on such a one-sided deal, so he made it in the form of an executive agreement instead of a treaty ratified by the Senate. Had Obama secured a ratified treaty with Iran, no future president could have broken it. This gave President Trump the option of abrogating the agreement with the stroke of a pen.

In February 2017, in response to illegal Iranian missile tests, Trump imposed new sanctions on more than two dozen Iranian individuals and companies that had been involved in procuring the banned ballistic missile technology. He subsequently imposed numerous crippling economic sanctions on Iran's government as well.

Finally, in May 2018, in the face of opposition from the entire Democratic Party and the European Union, Trump formally withdrew the United States from the treacherous Iran Nuclear Deal.

Foreign Policy: Syria

President Obama had infamously drawn a "red line" in the sand to stop Syria's dictator Assad from using chemical weapons on his own people. When Assad defied his threat and used the outlawed weapons, Obama did nothing, humiliating his country and himself. He did this in part in deference to the Iranians who were supporting the Assad regime. By contrast, four months into his presidency, Trump ordered a devastating missile strike against a Syrian airfield three days after the Khan Shaykhun chemical gas attack that killed 89 innocent people and injured over 500 more. Trump's response was an important departure in U.S. foreign policy, resulting in new respect for American power.

After the Syrian government again used chemical weapons on its people the following year, Trump—in coordination with France and England—ordered precision missile strikes on military installations in Syria. One hundred and five missiles successfully struck all three targets and crippled Syria's chemical weapons program.

In December 2018, President Trump signed the Iraq and Syria Genocide Relief and Accountability Act, which ensured that U.S. aid to the Middle East would reach Christians and other religious minorities. Where Obama's timidity had created a power vacuum in the Middle East that Russia and Iran filled, Trump's actions reminded the region that America was still a force to be reckoned with.

The War on Islamic Terrorism

After the attacks of 9/11 President George Bush described terrorism as an "existential threat" and declared a "Global War on Terror." His successor, Barack Obama, was in denial that radical Islam had launched a *jihad* or "holy war" against America. Soon after taking office, he sent a presidential message to senior Pentagon staff explaining that "this administration prefers to avoid using the term Long War or Global War On Terror (GWOT) . . . please pass this on to your speechwriters." Obama then replaced "war on terror" with the bureaucratic phrase "overseas contingency operations."[216] The attitude reflected in this change led directly to Obama's withdrawal from Iraq, the rise of ISIS, and the establishment of the Islamic state and caliphate.

In 2017, Trump's new national security strategy restored words relevant to understanding Islamic terrorism—such as *jihad*—that Obama had expunged from the Intelligence and Defense communities' lexicon. According to Trump's new strategy document, "The primary transnational threats Americans face are from *jihadist* terrorists and transnational criminal organizations." The document also vowed to "pursue threats to their source, so that *jihadist* terrorists are stopped before they ever reach our borders."[217] Trump himself used the phrase "radical Islamic terrorism" to describe America's enemy.

Still in denial as to the existence of an Islamic holy war against the West, Obama vowed to close the Guantanamo Bay detention center, which housed *jihadist* terrorists. He never was able to muster the political support to do so—though he did reduce the number of Guantanamo inmates from 245 to 41 (some were transferred, others were freed, and some returned to the battlefield to kill again). Trump understood the Islamic threat and issued an executive order to keep Guantanamo open.

In October 2018, Trump signed the Hezbollah International Financing Prevention Amendments Act. This law imposed sanctions not only on Hezbollah, but also on anyone found to be cooperating with the terrorist organization.

In January 2018, the United States withheld $255 million in military aid to Pakistan because of its noncooperation with U.S. counterterrorism efforts. America also suspended $900 million in security assistance to Pakistan. And in September 2018, the Trump administration permanently canceled $300 million in coalition support funds to Pakistan.

Obama had allowed ISIS and its depraved leader, Abu Bakr al-Baghdadi, to emerge from the ashes of the Iraq War, and to create a caliphate and establish the Islamic state in a territory as large as Ohio. While ISIS terrorists slaughtered hundreds of thousands of Syrians and Iraqis and created millions of refugees, Obama dithered, held back on using military force, and botched a chance to kill the ISIS leader.[218]

By contrast, from day one of his presidency, Trump made the destruction of the ISIS caliphate and the demise of its sadistic leader "the top national security priority of my administration."[219] In Trump's first year in office, the caliphate and Islamic state were destroyed, and on October 26, 2019, al-Baghdadi himself was hunted down and killed in a daring raid in northwestern Syria by U.S. forces under Trump's command.

How did the anti-Trump Democrats and their media allies respond to this victory? It was accomplished in Joe Biden's malicious words, "in spite of [Trump's] actions."[220]

Russia

In February 2017, newly inaugurated President Trump was being daily accused by Democrats of collusion with Russian dictator Vladimir Putin. At the same time, the Trump administration was actually initiating a series of get-tough measures to confront Russia. The United States launched a Russian-language TV network, *Current Time*, to counter Russian propaganda.[221] Two months later, the Trump administration announced it was implementing the Global Magnitsky Human Rights Accountability Act, which blacklisted prominent Russians who violated human rights.[222] In April 2017, the Trump administration refused to issue waivers to companies seeking to do business with Russia, which was under economic sanctions.[223]

In December 2017, the Trump administration approved the export of lethal small arms to Ukraine—something the Obama administration had refused to do—to support the country in its conflict with Russia-backed separatists. In August 2018, the U.S. Navy reestablished the Second Fleet in response to increased Russian activity in the north Atlantic Ocean. In February 2019, the Trump administration announced that the United States would withdraw from the Intermediate-Range Nuclear Forces Treaty due to Russia's repeated and persistent violations of the pact. The United States officially withdrew from the Treaty in August 2019.

The Corrupt United Nations

Trump also took on the terror-supporting, Israel-bashing United Nations. He withdrew the United States from the UN Human Rights Council, which regularly singled out America's democratic ally for condemnation while ignoring the atrocities committed against Jewish civilians by Hamas, Hezbollah, and other Iran-sponsored terrorist organizations. In June 2018, the Trump administration announced that it would leave the UN Human Rights Council because of its anti-Israel bias. This made America the first country ever to leave the Council.

In April 2017, the Trump administration ended U.S. funding of the UN Population Fund, which had links to China's policy of restricting its citizens to one child only.[224] In October 2017, the Trump administration announced that the United States would withdraw from UNESCO because of its anti-Israel hatred.[225]

In December 2017, the Trump administration pulled out of the Global Compact on Migration, a United Nations agreement that infringed upon U.S. sovereignty and its immigration policies. In January 2018, the Trump administration announced that it would withhold $65 million of a scheduled $125 million payment to the UN Relief and Works Agency (UNRWA) that UN officials had earmarked for Palestinian terrorists. That same month, the State Department announced America would withhold an additional $45 million that had been slated for Palestinian terrorists as well.[226]

In August 2018, the Trump administration announced that it would permanently defund UNRWA, which was notorious for running Palestinian refugee camps as training sites for terrorists.[227]

Policy Toward Israel

Israel had been the target of unprovoked Arab aggression since 1948, but U.S. presidents tried to approach the Middle East conflict as a neutral arbiter—until Trump's election. Three previous U.S. presidents had promised to move the American Embassy in Israel to Jerusalem, the capital of the Jewish state and the historic center of Judaism. But none had the courage to fulfill their promise because they feared reprisals from the Arabs. At the end of his first year in office, Trump did what his predecessors had lacked the courage to do and moved the American embassy to Jerusalem.

In contrast to Obama, who was hostile toward Israel's leader and critical of the Jewish state, Trump voiced a clear, unambiguous support for the only democracy in the Middle East. Five months into his presidency, Trump became the first sitting U.S. president ever to visit the Western Wall, Judaism's holiest site.

In August 2018, the Trump administration announced it would cut over $200 million in aid to the Palestinians, because of their support for terror and unwillingness to engage in peace talks with the Jews.[228] The Palestinians refused to cease these activities because their overt goal since 1948 had been the destruction of the Jewish state—a genocide, not a negotiated peace. In September 2018, the Trump administration closed the PLO's mission in Washington because of the Palestinians' continuing support for terrorism and belligerence toward the Jews.[229]

In November 2018, instead of abstaining, as on previous occasions, the United States voted against an annual UN resolution demanding that Israel withdraw from the Golan Heights, from which the Syrians had shelled Jewish cities until Israel responded by occupying them. In March 2019, Trump signed a proclamation officially recognizing the Golan Heights as part of Israel.[230]

In April 2018, the State Department's annual human rights report removed the phrases "occupied" and "occupation" when referring to Israel's presence in the West Bank—a presence that had always been necessitated by Arab aggressions, and by the Arabs' determination to "obliterate" the Jewish state.[231] The following year Trump declared the Jewish settlements in the West Bank to be legal, underscoring the fact that every inch of territory occupied by Arabs in the West Bank is the fruit of unprovoked aggression and failed conquest.[232]

Protecting America's Borders

Trump launched his presidential campaign by expressing his concerns about the security of America's borders, without which he said a nation cannot exist. He was alarmed by the flood of unvetted, *illegal* immigrants pouring across America's southern border, among whom were terrorists, drug and sex traffickers, and common criminals, whom he saw as threats to the security of ordinary Americans. To deal with a problem that had been festering for decades, he proposed extending the existing security wall, which would allow America's border guards to deal with the hundreds of thousands of migrants seeking illegal entry into the country.

When Democrats refused to cooperate in funding the wall, he found ways to make up the deficit.

In his first year, Trump authorized raids to apprehend members of the vicious gang MS-13, which preyed on Hispanic communities in the United States In that same year, ICE's Homeland Security Investigations division arrested 796 MS-13 members and associates—an 84 percent increase over the last year of the Obama administration.[233]

In 2019 Trump's policies led to the arrests of over one million individuals attempting to enter the country illegally.[234] At the same time, according to the State Department, Trump's travel bans from terrorist countries, which were eventually upheld by the Supreme Court, prevented more than thirty thousand people from entering the country, among whom there could have been any number of terrorists.[235]

Caring for America's Veterans

On Veteran's Day 1994 in New York City, soldiers, sailors, airmen, and Marines marched along Fifth Avenue, from 39th Street to Madison Square Park. Yet the street was largely empty and the parading veterans received few cheers or salutes. Interest in the parade was so low that organizers counted only a hundred spectators along the entire parade route.

The following year, Donald Trump donated $200,000 and helped raise an additional $300,000 from his friends to increase community awareness and involvement in the parade. When the 1995 parade was held, police estimated at least half a million people were on hand, cheering and waving flags. Vietnam veteran and parade director Tom Fox said, "Donald Trump saved the parade."[236]

The cause of honoring and caring for American's veterans has always been close to Trump's heart. So when he launched his presidential bid in 2015, one of the first promises he made was to end the scandalous treatment of American heroes by the Veterans Health Administration.

Trump was deeply disturbed by the 2014 news story of systematic neglect and abuse of America's veterans by the Veterans Health Administration (VHA). Patients died waiting for appointments while bureaucrats and administrators falsified records to collect fat "merit pay" bonuses. The Obama administration promised a shakeup at the VHA, including firings of bad employees—but the *New York Times* found that at most three bad employees were removed. More than a hundred employees were "disciplined" by merely being moved to another facility or, worse, being placed on paid leave—an indefinite paid vacation at taxpayer expense for bad behavior.

On April 27, 2017—three months after taking office—President Trump signed Executive Order 13793 to improve accountability and make it easier to fire bad employees at the VHA. By Veterans Day 2019, this order had resulted in the firing of more than 8,000 lazy, corrupt, or incompetent Veterans Affairs employees.

Speaking to a seniors group in Florida in October 2019, Trump said, "Do you remember all of the bad stories that used to be about the VA? Now you don't see that because they have accountability. We can fire bad people. We fired a tremendous number of really bad people that should've been fired years ago. I don't like firing people, but I like firing people that don't treat our vets great, that aren't doing their job."[237]

In June 2019 Trump signed the Veterans Affairs (VA) Missions Act, for which he had lobbied hard. Though the signing went unnoticed by the media, it was the most sweeping change in veterans' health care since World War II. As Secretary of Veterans Affairs Robert Wilkie explained, "If it's too long a drive to the VA, if wait times are too long, if we can't offer the services a veteran needs, or if it's simply in the best medical interest of a veteran to use non-VA services, they can now seek care in their community"—and the VHA will pay the bills.[238]

Because of Trump's reforms, in 2019 the department achieved the highest patient satisfaction rating in its history—89.7 percent.[239]

A Record American Economy

Securing the borders and protecting the country were Trump's first priorities, but rebuilding the American economy was a close second. America's manufacturing industry had been decimated through imprudent trade deals under previous presidents. From the beginning of his campaign, Trump promised to rectify the situation and revive the manufacturing sector that had been lost to unfair trade arrangements. Even before Trump secured the Republican nomination, President Obama called him out on this promise and said it was impossible to fulfill.

"During a PBS town hall, . . ." reported *The Hill* newspaper, ". . . Obama referenced Trump's promise to bring back jobs to the United States when talking about manufacturing. 'Well, how exactly are you going to do that? What exactly are you going to do? There's no answer to it,' Obama said. '[Trump] just says, well I'm going to negotiate a better deal. Well, what, how exactly are you going to negotiate that? What magic wand do you have?'"[240]

What Obama found so impossible he didn't even try to rectify, Trump did. From day one in office, Trump pursued efforts that were successful, magic wand or no. During his first 30 months in the White House, 499,000 manufacturing jobs were created, the fastest rate of growth in more than 30 years.[241]

To unleash the forces of the American economy, Trump set his sights on paring down the size of the federal government. He signed an executive order instituting a federal hiring freeze, and a government-wide review of every executive agency and department to find out, "where money is being wasted [and] how services can be improved."

He scaled back federal regulations that had been choking business investment. He enacted regulatory relief for community banks and credit unions. And he lifted a fourteen-month-old Obama-imposed moratorium on new coal leases on federal lands, causing U.S. coal exports to increase by 60 percent.

He also withdrew the United States from the Paris Climate Accord, under which the United States was required to shoulder the lion's share of the burdens with no tangible environmental benefits because China and India, the world's two largest polluters, were not required to control emissions under the agreement since they were "developing nations." They merely had to pledge to do so. The incentive for China and India to sign was that they get in line to receive billions of dollars in largesse from the West, especially the United States.

They have everything to gain and nothing to lose by signing the Paris Agreement. The United States has everything to lose and nothing to gain, which is why Trump walked away.[242]

In 2018, Trump signed a record tax cut. The bill provided more than $5.5 trillion in gross tax cuts, nearly 60 percent of which went to families. His bill doubled the child tax credit and nearly doubled the standard deduction for individuals and families.[243] In addition, he dramatically lowered America's corporate tax rate from the highest in the developed world to a level where American corporations could compete with their foreign competitors.

In addition, Trump issued executive orders to fast-track governmental approval for the construction of the Dakota Access and Keystone XL Oil Pipelines, previously blocked by the Obama administration. When Obama left office, 94 percent of the outer continental shelf had been off-limits to drilling. In 2018 Trump announced a five-year plan to open up all offshore drilling areas to leasing—in the Gulf, the Atlantic, the Pacific, and the Alaskan coast.[244]

As a direct consequence of Trump's measures, the United States is now energy independent and is the world's largest producer of crude oil—facts that have dramatic implications for America's national security and economic health.

During the 2016 election campaign, President Obama called Trump's pledge to roll back economic regulations "crazy," telling viewers of the PBS town hall: "That will not help us win. That is not going to make your lives better."[245]

Actually, it did. The results of Trump's policies have been the creation of the most prosperous American economy ever.

In three years in office, Trump has presided over an economic boom that has lifted people of all demographic groups. For the first time in history, most new hires between the ages of twenty-five and fifty-four are nonwhites. In 2018, the national poverty rate fell to 11.8 percent, the lowest annual figure since 2001. At the same time, median household income reached the highest level ever recorded.[246]

In September 2019, the overall unemployment rate nationwide (as reported by the Bureau of Labor Statistics) was 3.5 percent, while the black and Hispanic unemployment rates were at all-time lows, and the Asian unemployment rate was at its lowest level since 2003. Women's unemployment was at its lowest level in sixty-five years. Youth unemployment was at its lowest level in nearly fifty years. Between January 2017 and August 2019, the total number of people employed nationwide increased by 5.75 million.

According to the Agriculture Department, between February 2017 and the summer of 2019, a total of 6,268,285 individuals were able to discontinue their dependence on the food stamp program.[247]

As of July 30, 2019, the stock market was valued at $31.7 trillion, an increase of approximately $8 trillion in two and a half years.[248]

By way of comparison, in eight years Bush raised the median American income $400. Over the same time span, Obama raised median incomes $1,000. But in less than three years Trump raised the median income of Americans $4,144—an amount that increases by about $1,400 when the tax cuts are factored in.[249]

Leader of a Free Nation

At least as important as these material and foreign policy achievements was Trump's leadership on the cultural front. First and foremost was his championing of religious freedom.

Religious freedom—enshrined in the First Amendment—is the foundation of all America's freedoms. For decades it has been under siege by the secular left.[250] Before his election, Trump announced he would select a conservative to take the seat vacated by the death of Justice Antonin Scalia. This was a signal to the evangelical community that Trump was committed to stopping the series of anti-religious—and unconstitutional—Supreme Court rulings that abridged religious freedom. These tragic rulings began with the 1962 bans on prayer and Bible reading, and eventually led to the removal of all reference to Judeo-Christian ideas and values in the nation's public schools and public squares.

As one of his first acts, Trump appointed conservative Judge Neil Gorsuch to the Court and then Judge Brett Kavanaugh. The public lynching of Kavanaugh by congressional Democrats during his confirmation process demonstrated just how deep the fault lines were regarding these basic freedoms, and how important it was to have a president who would not back down when it came to defending them. Trump eventually appointed more than 200 federal judges who could be expected to honor the Constitution as its framers intended.

The Obama administration had supported a series of suits designed to deny religious freedom to groups like the Little Sisters of the Poor by forcing them to distribute contraceptives in violation of their beliefs. The policy was declared unconstitutional by the Supreme Court in 2016. The following year Trump reversed Obama's anti-religious course by filing a brief supporting the Colorado baker who refused to make a wedding cake endorsing gay marriage because it would be against his faith. While the Obama-supported suit nearly destroyed the baker's business, it was finally declared unconstitutional by the Supreme Court in June 2018.

Despite the attacks from the left over these decisions, Trump was actually far more "liberal" than the LGBTQ organizations that harassed the baker and tried to destroy his business. This was manifest in Trump's support for a global campaign to end the criminalization of homosexuality.[251]

In 2018 Trump also became the first sitting president to speak at the annual March for Life and support the rights of unborn children, more than sixty million of whom had been killed since *Roe v. Wade*.

As a powerful advocate for diversity of thought and the First Amendment, Trump was a strong supporter of the Second Amendment. The Founders incorporated this amendment into the Bill of Rights in order to provide for the defense of individuals against oppressive government and individual predators. Three months into his presidency, Trump declared: "The eight-year assault on your Second Amendment freedoms has come to a crashing end. . . . No longer will the government be trying to undermine your rights and your freedoms as Americans."[252]

Trump also seized the torch in the battle against the corrosive anti-Americanism that for decades had attempted to make patriotism a suspect loyalty. When professional football players egged on by radical activists "took a knee" during the national anthem and the presentation of the American flag, Trump emerged as their foremost and most powerful critic. His trademark slogans—"Make America Great Again" and "America First"—were the banners under which a national resistance to such disrespect was formed.

Leader of a Diverse and Inclusive Nation

Finally, Trump embraced minority constituencies and led a bipartisan alliance on behalf of a prison reform bill to correct injustices to African Americans. These injustices had been created by the 1994 crime bill signed into law by President Clinton. The reform had been a priority for America's African American community for a long time, but was ignored for sixteen years by the Bush and Obama administrations. Trump put together a bipartisan coalition to pass the reform.

Far-left activist and CNN commentator Van Jones characterized Trump's success in getting the "First Step Act" passed in these terms: "There is a Christmas miracle underway. For the first time in a generation, Republicans and Democrats are arm-in-arm tonight saying we are sending too many people to prison. . . . Hakeem Jeffries on the left, Jared Kushner and Donald Trump on the right, have brought together a coalition like I have never seen. . . . [S]omething beautiful is happening and it is not that you have to see it to believe it, you have to believe it to see it. It is happening right now, people coming together to help the people who have nothing. And it is amazing."[253]

In August 2019, the NAACP released the results of a poll that showed the impact of Trump's overtures. It registered a 21 percent approval rating for Trump among African

Americans, more than double the approval registered in a Reuters poll conducted in April. In reporting these results, however, the NAACP went into denial mode to portray Trump as still anti-black: "Voters across all racial and ethnic groups believe Trump is setting race relations back," the organization claimed in its poll analysis. These were voters listening to Democrats like Bernie Sanders who was telling audiences on the campaign trail at that very moment, "We've got a president right now who is a racist."[254]

On September 10, eleven days before Sander's slander, Trump addressed a conference of Historically Black Colleges and Universities (HBCU) in Washington, D.C., and explained what his administration had done for them. "For more than 180 years," Trump said, "HBCUs have strengthened our country and called America to greatness. Your institutions have been pillars of excellence in higher education and the engines of advancement for African-American citizens. That is why, in my first weeks in office, I took action to make HBCUs a top priority once again. I signed an executive order to move the federal HBCU initiative to the White House, right where it belongs. . . . I signed legislation to increase federal funding for HBCUs by a record 13 percent. That was the highest ever done. . . . In total, over the last two and a half years, through the Capital Financing Program, we have provided more than $500 million in loans to HBCUs." On December 19, 2019 Trump signed a bi-partisan bill that would restore $250 million to HBCUs.

"Every day of my presidency," Trump said, "we'll strive to give every child, of every background and every race, religion, and creed, the best chance to reach that beautiful American

Dream."[255] It was a credo he put his resources, his leadership talents and his presidency behind, while his opponents continued their campaign to defame him as a racist and impeach him.

14

The MAGA President's War

DONALD TRUMP IS THE scion of a German-American immigrant family. His grandfather, Friedrich Trump, came to the United States from Bavaria in 1885, virtually penniless and without a profession. Friedrich's son Fred became a hugely successful real estate developer, amassing a fortune of several hundred million dollars before his death in 1999. Fred's son Donald carried on the Trump success story, becoming a billionaire and television celebrity in his own right before being elected president of the United States.

No one looking at Trump's career in a fair-minded manner can fail to see that his driving political ambition for twenty years—from the time he first tested the presidential waters in 2000—was a patriotic desire to restore American prosperity and strength, and to make America live up its promise. He chafed at the bad trade deals that both Republican and Democrat presidents had signed, which provided trillions of dollars in subsidies to countries like China, Mexico, and Japan. He objected to the regulations that hamstrung American businesses and kept America's growth rates low, unemployment rates high, and food stamp rolls expanding. He was concerned at how the previous Democrat administration had degraded America's military, while providing more than $150 billion in support to America's mortal enemy, Iran.

In his 2000 campaign book, *The America We Deserve*, Trump laid out his political vision, which included strengthening America as a diverse, inclusive, multiracial nation by expanding opportunity for all. It is a credo that belies the vicious slanders which the Democrat Party and the hate-Trump crowd have relentlessly leveled against him.

"I believe in the American Dream," Trump wrote. "My business experience shows me that it works, and I want to do everything possible to see that regular Americans can enjoy the same opportunity for success and security that I have had. That means the American Dream unencumbered by bureaucratic ineptitude, government regulation, confiscatory tax policies, racism, discrimination against women, or discrimination against people based on sexual orientation. We must all have equal access to the American Dream. It's a dream we deserve and a dream worth fighting for."[256] To this he added: "When you mess with the American Dream, you're on the fighting side of Trump."[257]

This credo explains his antagonism toward a progressive left that has openly rejected the American Dream in favor of a racist identity politics, and a "fundamental transfor-mation" of America into a socialist state. In his 2019 State of the Union address, which effectively launched his 2020 campaign, Trump swore, "We were born free and we will stay free. . . . America will never be a socialist country."[258]

Given the socialist goals of the leftists who took control of the Democrat Party under Obama, it is not surprising the Democrats created an unprecedented Resistance to Trump's presidency. For the past half century or more, we have wit-nessed the far left infiltrating America's mainstream in what they describe as "the long march through the institutions."[259] According to a founding father of modern Marxism, Antonio Gramsci, the overthrow of the existing social order will be achieved by gradually infiltrating and controlling the cul-ture-creating institutions of society—the very institutions that form the power base of the left's anti-Trump Resistance: schools, universities, the media, the literary and arts commu-nities, philanthropies, the so-called "rights coalition," the "public sector" trade unions, and large swaths of the judi-ciary and legal professions. This "long march" was well on its way to reaching its goal—until the election of 2016.[260]

In that referendum the Resistance met an irresistible force in the person of Donald Trump.

The Fog of Hatred

Again and again, the Democrats have tried to sabotage and defeat Trump—yet again and again they have failed. Why? There is one central defect that pervades all anti-Trump strat-egies, and it is this: Leftists are unable to see through the fog of their own hatred. This prevents them from understanding

Trump, understanding his supporters, and understanding how they themselves are viewed by others. They do not even see how contradictory and irrational their views of Trump are.

Years into Trump's presidency they continue to portray him as a ruthless Hitlerian dictator *and* as a bumbling incompetent. Well, which is it? Because he can't be both. They tell us that Trump wants to "make America white again." Well, where is the evidence for this slander? After several years in office, they should be able to point to his "racist" or "white supremacist" policies. Yet by every objective standard, Americans of every race and ethnicity are faring much better under Trump than they did under Obama.

It is one thing to raise extreme fears of what a candidate might do if he should win office and gain the power to affect the future. But it is quite another to stoke those same fears after he has been in office several years and done so much to improve people's lives.

Even when Trump's opponents charge him with wicked policies, rather than unpleasant character defects, they can't seem to prevent their visceral hatred from running far in advance of the obvious facts. For weeks at a time in the summer of 2019, a major Democratic theme was Trump's "un-American" and "inhumane" policy of separating illegal immigrant children from their parents and caging them at the border in conditions that anti-Semitic Democrats like Ocasio-Cortez and Ilhan Omar cynically described as reminiscent of the Nazi concentration camps during the Holocaust.

"It's a human rights abuse," agreed Senator Kamala Harris in the most self-righteous accents she could summon. To support their accusations, the Democrats produced photos of fenced-in children as proof of Trump's evil actions. But it turned out that the photos came from the Obama era, and those "cages" (and the policies that produced them) belonged to Barack Obama. Moreover, it was the refusal of current Democrats (including Harris and Cortez) to work with Trump to change the immigration laws that forced this unhappy interim solution.

Harris had previously called Trump a "white supremacist who has no empathy," a sentiment echoed by many Democrats.[261] Apparently, the senator and her colleagues were asleep when Trump went out of his way to get an African-American grandmother, Alice Johnson, released from prison where she had served twenty-one years of a life sentence for nonviolent drug trafficking. If Senator Harris hadn't been blinded by hate, she could have celebrated Trump's signing of the First Step Act, a prison reform law that released thousands of African American felons from jail for a second chance in life. Trump's compassionate gestures are even more impressive when contrasted with the failure of his predecessor, Barack Obama, to take such actions during his eight years in office.

The 2020 Democratic presidential candidates all accused Trump of being a "white supremacist," indicting his sixty-three million supporters in the process. But by deploying these charges repetitively and recklessly, progressives cheapened and diminished them. Only a few years ago, to be labeled a racist was as abhorrent as being labeled a pedophile. But progressives have accused so many decent, innocent Americans of racism that outside the left this charge has largely lost its sting.

Increased Attacks, Decreased Impact

The Democrats' failed attempt to bludgeon Trump to political death has forced them to ramp up their attacks, weakening their case even further. During the 2016 campaign, Hillary Clinton infamously insulted *half* of Trump's base, saying, "You could put half of Trump's supporters into what I call the basket of deplorables. Right? The racist, sexist, homophobic, xenophobic, Islamophobic—you name it." That's bad enough—but by the fall of 2019, presidential aspirant Pete Buttigieg, and other Democratic candidates, and their media cheering section were brazenly labeling *all* Trump supporters "racists."

Buttigieg's comments came up in the third Democrat primary debate when he was asked a loaded question by Univision's Jorge Ramos, a Trump hater and prominent advocate of open borders. The question was about Trump's immigration policies: "President Trump has called Mexican immigrants rapists and killers, tried to ban Muslims from entering the country, and separated children from their parents. His supporters have chanted, 'build the wall' and 'send them back.' Do you think that people who support President Trump and his immigration policies are racist?"[262]

Trump has never called Mexican *immigrants* "rapists and killers," or tried to ban Muslims from entering the country. He has never ordered children separated from their parents. Such separations are merely routine procedure whenever parents are arrested for breaking any laws, including immigration laws. It's standard American policy not to put entire families in jail for parental transgressions.

But Pete Buttigieg accepted Ramos's false premise and insulted all Trump supporters by saying, "Anyone who supports this [Trump's stance on *illegal* immigration] is supporting racism."

The anti-Trump rhetoric from the Democrats and their media allies has poisoned the public atmosphere to the point where a rational, fact-based discourse about illegal immigration has become impossible. Even a quasi-academic organization like the Brookings Institution could not produce a report on the issue without relying on deceptive language and a blatantly false premise.

The opening sentence of the Brookings report speaks of "the role President Trump's racist rhetoric has played in encouraging violence in America" as if these were self-evident facts. To underpin these malicious claims, the report conflates legal and *illegal* immigrants, erasing any distinction between the two. Because Trump opposes *illegal* immigration, according to Brookings, he must be a racist. In normal speak, that would be someone who opposes immigration by "people of color." But Trump does not oppose immigration by nonwhites. From this false premise, the Brookings authors proceed to impute racist motives to all Trump supporters who wish only to enforce American immigration laws and secure America's borders.[263]

This kind of doublespeak overkill has numbed the senses of those making such charges to the point where they fail to realize how their deceptions actually serve to undermine their efforts to demonize Trump and his followers. It's a problem that inevitably arises when one sets out to kill the messenger rather than refute the message.

The Impeachable Offense Is Trump Himself

After nearly three years in office, Trump was a well-known quantity. He had a record of accomplishments that made it increasingly hard for his opponents to redefine and defame him. Those who attempted to caricature Trump as a monster were forced to employ increasingly absurd rhetoric and logic. Democrats and their allies had already regularly compared Trump to Hitler and Stalin, but he remained standing. So Brian Stelter, the host of CNN's misnamed "*Reliable Sources*" invited a psychiatrist named Dr. Allen Frances on his show to make the following claim: "Trump is as destructive a person in this century as Hitler, Stalin, and Mao were in the last century. He may be responsible for many more million deaths than they were."[264]

For the record, Hitler, Stalin, and Mao were responsible for well over 200 million deaths. Stelter, who is CNN's "chief media correspondent," let the outrageous slander pass without comment, showing just how corrupt the anti-Trump "news" networks have become. Later, when called out for his silence, Stelter pretended he hadn't heard what the doctor said. But it's far more likely that the reason Dr. Frances was invited on Stelter's show in the first place was because he was prepared to make that ridiculous and hateful charge.

The Democrats presented their relentless, multiyear quest for an impeachable offense as a pursuit of justice. But to Americans not committed to the Democrats' vendetta, the grasping after impeachment straws was more reminiscent of Beria's infamous assurance to Stalin: "Show me the man, and I'll find you the crime."[265]

The desperate pursuit of a pretext with which to hang Trump diminished the very meaning of what an impeachable offense might be. It obviously wasn't a particular offense that inspired the Democrats' fishing expedition. After all, they trotted out a new and different impeachment pretext on a monthly, even weekly basis. It was Trump himself who was the impeachable offense. The impeachment campaign was an effort to circumvent the electoral process, which is the cornerstone of America's democratic order.

In her opening statement at a primary debate in Charleston, South Carolina, Senator Kamala Harris threw down this gauntlet to the president, who, she said, "we all know is watching."

> President Trump, you've spent the last two and a half years full-time trying to sow hate and division among us. You have used hate, intimidation, fear, and over 12,000 lies as a way to distract from your failed policies and your broken promises. What you don't get is that the American people are so much better than this and we know that the vast majority of us have so much more in common than what separates us, regardless of our race, where we live, or the party with which we're registered to vote.[266]

It would be hard to top the sanctimonious arrogance of this statement. Kamala Harris is one of the most rancorous members of a party that had been ginning up outrageous slanders against Trump and his supporters since even before the 2016 vote was counted. Though Harris piously accused

Trump of waging a verbal war of hate, she and her fellow Democrats had repeatedly denounced Trump as a racist, a white supremacist, a putative dictator "unfit" for the office, mentally unstable, and incompetent—divisive lies all. When did Kamala Harris ever try to reach out to Trump and his supporters? When did these anti-Trump critics ever emphasize what Democrats and Republicans have in common in order to unify the nation? When did they do anything but vilify and demonize Trump and the sixty-three million Americans who voted for him?

In its war against Trump, the Democrat Party has itself become a party of hate, accusing Trump and his supporters of racism for as innocent a desire as to see America's immigration laws enforced. If Americans are divided it is the Democrats' collective decision to demonize their opponents and lie about what they stand for that is the source of the division.

A War We Ignore at Our Peril

At the same Democrat primary debate in which Harris challenged Trump, former congressman Beto O'Rourke joined the hate chorus with this rant: "We have a white supremacist in the White House, and he poses a mortal threat to people of color all across this country." O'Rourke then went a bridge further, making it clear that he did not at all agree with Congressman Al Green's view that Trump should be impeached because he was *unfit* to represent American values. On the contrary, according to O'Rourke, Trump was *perfectly fit* to represent them, because America itself was a racist threat to people of color. According to O'Rourke, America was, in fact, a nation that in its origins and in its essence was dedicated to the proposition that people of color were unequal and destined to be abused:

> Racism in America is endemic. It is foundational. We can mark the creation of this country not at the 4th of July, 1776, but August 20, 1619, when the first kidnapped African was brought to this country against his will. And in bondage, and as a slave, built the greatness and the success and the wealth that neither he nor his descendants would ever be able to fully participate in and enjoy.[267]

Let us first correct the ignorance and racism of this familiar rant, which begins by ascribing *English* slavery that prevailed on the North American continent from 1619 *until* the United States of America was created in 1787 to the new nation that abolished it. The United States was founded on the principles of equality and liberty for all. From the moment of its founding Americans began freeing their slaves—some 500,000 by the early 1800s—and in 1808 outlawed the slave trade entirely. If they had abolished slavery in the South as well in that year, the British, who burned the White House in 1812, would have joined the slave states in a war to crush the North, preserving the slave system for who knows how long.

Also, let us once again correct the falsehood that black Africans were "kidnapped" by white Americans into slavery, as the historically illiterate O'Rourke claims. In fact, they were *bought* from black African slave owners at slave auctions in Ghana and Benin. Finally, there is no evidence that the plantation economy of the slaveholding South created

American wealth. It was the greater productivity of the free industrial economy of the North that lay behind the Union's victory in the Civil War.

Based on such contempt for historical reality, presidential candidate O'Rourke's hatred for his own country is both visceral and repulsive. It is slander directed at America's heritage of freedom. What is essential to America's story from its origins is not racism but the dedication of the majority of its citizens to the ideals of liberty and equality, which have, over time, positively transformed the lives of millions of "people of color," not only in America but all over the world.

Unfortunately, this is not one man's self-hatred and traitorous malice. More disturbing than O'Rourke's anti-American venom is the fact that not one of the other nine Democrats beside him on the debate platform, nor the left-wing CNN moderators, nor the leftwing media pundits who reported the event, were offended by O'Rourke's statements, or thought to refute them. These America-hating remarks are worthy of America's most dangerous enemies. They are made worse by coming from a candidate seeking the office of America's commander-in-chief.

Equally alarming is the fact that O'Rourke's defamatory fiction—that America was founded in 1619 rather than 1776 or 1787—is drawn directly from the 1619 Project, which is the creation of the *New York Times* and the Pulitzer Center, two of America's leading cultural institutions. This anti-American propaganda will soon become the curriculum in America's K-12 schools where children will be indoctrinated in toxic anti-American views, while lacking the knowledge to refute them.

O'Rourke's slanders of his country and attacks on its heritage are hardly unique among the leadership of the Democratic Party. Three days before O'Rourke's repellent outburst, Congresswoman Rashida Tlaib tweeted the following poisonous call to her comrades: "We have to make the tough, courageous changes that completely transform a political and economic system that is now built for corporations (and profits), not people. Choosing the *status quo* means doing nothing and giving up. We need a political revolution."[268]

This historically illiterate Marxist attack on America is standard fare for so-called progressives and Democratic leaders. Leaders of the anti-American Democrats are Senator Bernie Sanders, a self-described socialist and a lifelong supporter of Communist causes, and his colleague Senator Elizabeth Warren, who masks her anti-American goals by calling for "big structural changes," which is merely code for the revolution she obviously desires.[269]

Her "big structural change" begins with the elimination of the American oil and gas industries, which would be a gift to America's Russian, Iranian, and Venezuelan enemies. Empowering America's enemies, however, doesn't seem to concern her. She also proposes eliminating the nation's private health insurance industry with its 180 million customers. She would replace the current system with a single-payer, Communist-style, government-controlled health care system. She plans a similar "big structural change" for public education, which she also wants to place entirely under the heel of the state.

Warren is a tireless spokesperson for the radicals who complain that capitalism "puts profits over people." The notion that profits are opposed to people is a measure of the economic ignorance of Warren and others like her. How does one build a business and earn a profit *without* satisfying human needs? How does an employer create jobs without earning profits? In the real world, profits are a measure of efficiency and value. Profits are an incentive for an entrepreneur to invest and put capital at risk. Profits are the measure of wealth creation for the investors who make these enterprises possible. Personal profit by serving human needs is the incentive that motivates workers to seek improvement of their own lives.

Free market capitalism is based on human freedom—the billions of individual, voluntary transactions made every day by buyers and sellers. It is based on mutual accommodation—I give you something of value, you give me something of value, and we both come away enriched by the exchange. These interactions provide incentives to invest and create. These incentives don't just move wealth around—they *create wealth*.

Read any page from the vast libraries of socialist literature, and you'll read nothing about the creation of wealth, but plenty about the *redistribution* of wealth by means of taxation or confiscation. Socialism involves the taking of wealth from one person *by force of government* and giving it to another. Bottom line: Socialism is theft. This is why, in socialist regimes, poverty invariably grows and wealth creation always diminishes.

America's incredible prosperity has been made possible by the profit system. The hostility to private property and free markets embodied in the Green New Deal, and the Democrat attacks on America's founding are a declaration of war on economic freedom—a war we ignore at our peril.

The Challenge We Face

Trump will not ignore the left's war on America. In his 2020 quest for a second term, his unifying theme will be patriotism—defending the system that creates American prosperity, respecting America's legacy of faith and freedom, and proclaiming America's true history as a nation "conceived in liberty and dedicated to the proposition that all men are created equal."

When America won the Cold War in 1991, it was a victory over a socialist empire that murdered more than a hundred million people, enslaved many hundreds of millions more, and reduced whole continents to life-deadening poverty.

Another recent American victory was the civil rights revolution that affirmed the equality of individuals and completed the promise of 1776 for justice and equality for all. American equality presumes that free individuals are judged by the content of their character and their achievements as individuals. American equality rejects the hierarchies of skin color and gender and group identity that have been embraced by the anti-Trump left and the Democrat Party.

When Trump launched his second presidential run, he positioned himself as a leader in what was shaping up as a rerun of the Cold War: "Here, in the United States, we are alarmed by new calls to adopt socialism in our country. America was founded on liberty and independence—not government coercion, domination, and control. We are born free, and we will stay free."

Americans are wedded to their liberties. They do not want government agents knocking on their doors and forcing them to give up their constitutional rights, which is what gun and automobile confiscations under Democrat mandates will require. They do not want to live under the conditions of a military mobilization, which the Green New Deal would impose. Americans do not want anyone—let alone strangers who have violated their borders—to be afforded a "fundamental human right" to free health care, housing, and education at their expense. It is not a human right to confiscate the earnings and property of others to pay for what are not actually "free" services. Americans don't want a government of self-righteous dictators imposing "revolutionary" changes through executive orders. Americans want their hard-won freedoms.

On December 9, 2019, the inspector general of the Department of Justice issued a damning report on abuses committed by the FBI in its efforts to obtain warrants to spy on the Trump campaign and then the Trump White House. According to IG Michael Horowitz, an Obama appointee, the FBI lied to the FISA court, concealed exculpatory evidence and failed to inform the judges that the Steele dossier on Trump, which formed the basis of the warrants, was financed by the Clinton campaign and the DNC and had also been discredited. In other words, IG Horowitz validated the White House claim that Donald Trump was the target of a deep state conspiracy to undo the results of the 2016 election and destroy his presidency. This criminal behavior by the FBI led directly to the appointment of Special Prosecutor Mueller and the two-year investigation of the president that failed to establish that he had colluded with Russia to rig the 2016 election.[270]

Despite this exoneration, nine days later—without discussing the IG report or assessing its implications—the House Democrats continued their three-year effort to undo the 2016 election by passing two articles impeaching the president for "high crimes and misdemeanors." The vote was extremely and unprecedentedly partisan with no Republicans voting in favor. The articles did not contain any of the crimes Democrats had previously alleged—including bribery, extortion, and emoluments.

In Article 1 the president was accused of "abuse of power," a charge so vague that it could be applied to any officeholder. Article 2 accused him of "obstruction of Congress" for invoking executive privilege to resist requests for White House witnesses—something virtually every president has done. The procedure for adjudicating these disputes rests with the courts. The Democrats did not appeal to the courts because in their rush to judgment they did not want to follow the constitutional procedure.

The day before the impeachment vote, the president sent a scathing letter to House Speaker Nancy Pelosi: "I write to express my strongest and most powerful protest against the partisan impeachment crusade being pursued by Democrats in the House of Representatives. . . . By proceeding with your invalid impeachment, you are violating your oaths of office. You are breaking your allegiance to the Constitution, and you are declaring open war on American Democracy."

From the beginning of the Resistance to Trump, Democrat attacks on the president have been attacks on America's foundations: resistance to the results of a fair and free election; abetting a deep state coup to undermine the presidency, and the pursuit of a transparently sham impeachment. All this added up to a campaign of baseless slanders against the nation's commander-in-chief, worthy of America's most determined enemies. Collectively these constitute the greatest crime against America committed by its own citizens since the Civil War.

The damaging effects of this sabotage—weakening the nation in the face of her enemies, obstructing the president's economic and social programs, defying the nation's immigration laws—are incalculable. Fortunately, in 2016 Americans elected a leader who has been able to withstand these seditious attacks and steer the nation forward, making it more prosperous and stronger than ever before in its history.

By his actions over the course of his first White House term, Donald Trump has shown Americans that in the war the Democrats have declared on him—and, through him, on their country—he can lead them to victory and secure a better future for all.

Afterword

The Nine Biggest Dangers to America
from the Anti-Trump Left

1. Resistance. A strategy that is opposed to the most basic principles and core freedoms on which America was built: freedom of conscience, freedom of speech, and the sovereignty of the people through a free vote.

"Resistance" is the rallying cry of enemies of America's political order, which is designed to encourage compromise and the settlement of conflicts through the ballot box. The Democrat Resistance, to Trump is funded by George Soros and his anti-American networks. It was launched with a deep state plot to spy on the Trump 2016 campaign and then concoct a Russia-collusion hoax to portray Trump as a traitor to his country. This was followed by a congressional strategy of obstruction to deny him a legislative agenda. Democrats then escalated the assault into a three-year partisan campaign to impeach and remove the president before the next election, nullifying both the 2016 and 2020 elections.

This Democrat assault on the electoral process includes its pre-Trump opposition to voter IDs that would protect the integrity of elections; calls to abolish the Electoral College and the U.S. Senate; and the granting of voting rights to illegal aliens.

2. Identity Politics. Identity politics is the commitment to an ideology that is collectivist and racist. It is a fundamental rejection of America's core commitments to individual freedom, accountability, and equality. It has led to the revival of the worst form of McCarthyism, which accuses the president without evidence of being a traitor, while indicting his supporters collectively as "racist, sexist, homophobic, Islamophobic" and "deplorable."

3. Open Borders. Democrat support for sanctuary cities and open borders constitutes a mortal threat to America's security and sovereignty. Support for illegal immigration displays a dangerous contempt for the very concept of American citizenship—a concept that includes sworn loyalty to country, respect for its laws and values, and commitment to its security and defense.

4. Green Communism. Under the guise of what its supporters describe as a "military mobilization" to defend the planet, Democrats propose a "Green New Deal" that would bankrupt the country, confiscate 267 million automobiles, force the restructuring of 300 million buildings destroy entire industries by "executive order," and make American energy dependent on Middle Eastern oil. The "Green New Deal" would establish a socialist dictatorship in which dissent from its agendas would be regarded as a threat not only to American security—treason—but to the survival of the planet itself.

5. Communist Health Care. The Democrats are dedicated to taking away Americans' basic freedom to choose their doctors and health care plans. They would put their life and death decisions—their fates—in the hands of a centralized state.

6. Support for Criminals and Contempt for the Law. Democrat coddling of violent criminals, including those in this country illegally is a well-established practice. In California and New York Democrats have already given their criminal populations "Get out of Jail Free" cards, while in hundreds of sanctuary cities they have broken the law to protect convicted felons, illegally in America, and prevented their deportation. At the same time, in equal disregard for the rule of law they have imposed draconian sentences for non-violent crimes on their political opponents.

7. Hostility to Religious Liberty and the First Amendment. These are the foundations of all American freedoms and they are under systematic assault by the political left. Already the institutions they dominate—the universities, the K–12 schools, the media—have witnessed the virtual outlawing of conservative thought and expression over the last twenty-five years. This is a direct result of an identity politics that demonizes dissent as "racist, sexist, homophobic, and Islamophobic."

8. Support for America's Enemies. Ever since the Democrats "Blame America First" convention in San Francisco in 1984, the party has steadily drifted to the left—the camp of appeasers and fifth-column supporters of America's enemies. Obama's rescue of the Iranian regime, which has killed thousands of Americans and is led by religious fanatics who chant "Death to America" is a policy that will live in infamy. Obama lifted sanctions on this regime, brought it out of its international isolation, provided it with a path to nuclear weapons, and gave it nearly 200 billion dollars in cash. This is the centerpiece of the treason Democrats are always flirting with, and which the war on Trump is a direct expression of. Conducting a three-year sabotage of the American presidency justified by a phony Russia-collusion hoax was an act of breathtaking treachery, which has done incalculable harm to America's security and that of her allies. Disloyalty at the highest levels promoted by the Democrat Party is now a danger Americans have to live with thanks to the takeover of that party by the anti-American left.

9. **Attack on America's Heritage.** The anti-Americanism of the Democrat Party and the liberal elites who support it has come to a head in the *New York Times'* sponsored 1619 Project, which seeks to discard America's historic role as a beacon of freedom with a myth central to the propaganda of America's enemies describing the freest most tolerant and inclusive nation as a "racist, white supremacist, predator defined not by its commitment to liberty but by a legacy of slavery," which in the words of Barack Obama is "part of America's DNA."

The Top Ten Lies the Democrats Have Told You

1. Republicans Are Racists—No, Democrats Are. Republicans are committed to America's traditional, constitutional values—equality and liberty for all, individual freedom and accountability, a society that judges individuals by the content of their character not the color of their skin. Ronald Reagan made Martin Luther King's birthday a national holiday, honoring him for this very reason. This is the opposite of racism. On the other hand, Democrats adhere to a racist philosophy called identity politics, which creates hierarchies based on race and gender. Democrats exercise monopoly control of America's major inner cities and killing fields—Chicago, Detroit, Baltimore, St. Louis, and so on and have done so for fifty to a hundred years. Every injustice and inequality in these cities, beginning with the failed public schools, which year in and year out fail to provide a basic education for 80 percent of their minority students, Democrats are 100 percent responsible for. This is true racism.

2. Democrats Care About Minorities—No, Democrats Care Only About Minority *Votes*. To secure their monopoly control of America's inner cities Democrats have created a class of minority bureaucrats—Cory Booker, Kamala Harris, the late Elijah Cummings, and Mazie Hirono are examples—whom they shower with benefits and powers, tasking them with keeping their captive constituencies in line. Their purpose is to ensure the continued electoral support of the minority victims of Democrat policies while the unconscionable conditions and carnage persist unchanged.

3. Republicans Betrayed the Constitution—No, Democrats Did. On September 24, 2019, House Speaker Nancy Pelosi announced that she was initiating formal impeachment proceedings against the president: "The actions of the Trump presidency have revealed the dishonorable fact of the president's betrayal of his oath of office, betrayal of our national security and betrayal of the integrity of our elections," Pelosi explained. The subsequent impeachment vote was passed on a strictly partisan basis—an unprecedented occurrence in the history of the country, and one that Pelosi herself had ruled out previously. The greatest fear of the framers of the Constitution was just this situation—the factionalism of political parties. Historically, democracies had been torn apart and destroyed by political factions. So, the founders created an elaborate system of checks and balances, to frustrate mob passions. These included the Electoral College and the undemocratic Senate both of which were designed to thwart the very factionalism that Pelosi was driving. Democrats' betrayal of the Constitution began before Trump's inauguration with their adoption of a strategy of Resistance to a duly elected president. This led to the "cold civil war" waged against Trump, leading to the collapse of what had been a three-year anticonstitutional effort to undo the results of the 2016 election.

4. Slavery and Racism Are America's True Heritage— No, Freedom Is. The anti-American hostilities of the progressive left can be seen most clearly—and most alarmingly—in the so-called 1619 Project, sponsored by the New York Times, the Pulitzer Foundation, and thousands of schools in all fifty states. The project is designed to deny America's founding was in 1776 or 1787. Instead according to these America detractors, this nation was founded in 1619 when twenty Africans were shipped to the English colony of Virginia. The purpose of the 1619 project is to demonstrate that "nearly everything that has made America exceptional grew out of slavery." In fact, slavery had existed for 3,000 years in all societies and was not declared immoral until the late eighteenth century when Wilberforce in England and Thomas Jefferson did so. Jefferson made the Declaration of Independence a revolutionary call for the equality of all human beings and for the God-given unalienable right to liberty for all as well—black slaves included. This led directly to the freedom of black slaves in all the northern states and then a civil war in which 350,000 mainly white union soldiers and an American president gave their lives for the freedom of their black brothers and sisters.

5. The Iran Deal Prevented Iran from Getting Nuclear Weapons—No, It Funded Their Terrorism and Financed Their Plans to Build Nuclear Weapons. In 1979 with the assistance of Democrat Jimmy Carter, Iran underwent a revolution that installed a fanatic Islamic regime to chants of

"Death to America." In the ensuing years, Iranian terrorists and IEDs killed thousands of Americans. Iran became the chief state sponsor of terror in the world. This led to sanctions designed to cripple its economy and isolate it from the international community. Then along came progressive Democrat Barack Obama who lifted the sanctions and brought Iran back into the community of nations. These moves led to the infamous Iran Nuclear Deal, which provided Iran with a guaranteed path to nuclear weapons and provided them with nearly $200 million in cash delivered on pallets in the middle of the night, facilitating the regime's ability to carry out terroristic activities throughout the Middle East. The Iran Nuclear deal was so treacherous that Obama did not dare present it for ratification to the US Senate but took it to the pro-terrorist UN for validation. The entire Democrat Party supported this treachery.

6. Donald Trump Colluded with the Russians—No, Democrats Did. The three-year effort to impeach Trump was based on a discredited dossier paid for by the Clinton campaign and the DNC, and put together by former British spy Christopher Steele and the Russian KGB. The $35 million two-year investigation by special prosecutor Mueller into the accusations against Trump found no evidence of any collusion between the president and the Russians. But this has not prevented Democrats like Rep. Eric Swalwell and MSNBC host—and professional liar—Lawrence O'Donnell from continuing to claim that "Trump is a Russian operative."

7. Republicans Are Religious Bigots—No, Democrats Are. Religious liberty enshrined in the First Amendment is the foundation of all American freedoms. It is why Americans have freedom of speech and freedom of assembly, without which they could not defend their other freedoms. Religious liberty consists of two parts: freedom of conscience and freedom of expression. Democrat religious bigots like Pete Buttigieg and the LGBTQ left recognize only the first. Their view of religious liberty is "you can believe anything you want but keep it to yourself. If you don't, we will harass and sue you out of existence."

8. The "Green New Deal" Is Scandinavian Socialism— No, It's Totalitarian Communism. In fact, the Scandinavian economies are capitalist, and the Green New Deal is more accurately described as "communist" not "democratic socialist." It's chief Democrat advocates, Bernie Sanders and Alexandria Ocasio-Cortez, are Marxist supporters of Communist and terrorist regimes. Their plans would require—by their own accounts—"a military mobilization." Its advocates promise the destruction of entire industries by executive order, the confiscation of 267 million automobiles, and a state takeover of the entire health care system—all paid for by astronomical taxes taken out of the pockets of every American to foot the $93 trillion bill for their pie-in-the-sky promises.

9. Israel Occupies Palestine—No, It Doesn't. This Is a Terrorist-Sponsored Genocidal Lie. Israel was created by the United Nations in the same way Syria, Jordan, Lebanon, and Iraq were created: out of the ruins of the Turkish Empire. Turks are not Arabs, let alone Palestinians. The Turks had ruled the territory known as the Palestine Mandate for over 400 years. Palestine Mandate is a geographical designation like New England. There has never been a political entity, "Palestine" or a people called "Palestinian." The identity

"Palestinian" was created in 1964 by the dictator Gamal Abdel Nasser, the KGB, and the PLO terrorists to make the Arabs look like victims instead of the terrorist aggressors they are.

10. Single-Payer Health Care Is a Human Right— No, Single-Payer Is a System That Destroys Individual Freedom. Single-payer health care is the takeover of health care and the crushing of individual freedom by the bureaucratic state. It removes from individuals the most important decisions over life and death, and is the end of privacy. Under single payer the state will have access to all personal records dealing with health and finances. This is the cornerstone of a communist dictatorship, which is why progressives embrace it. Health care is a privilege, not a "fundamental human right," unless one believes like communists that one person has a fundamental right to force another to pay for their health care, and to do so regardless of how recklessly they treat their bodies. Americans already enjoy the privilege of health care provided to them by a generous public. Better to add generosity to the system and keep individual freedom rather than turn it over to bureaucratic panels that will decide who gets what care and when, and also whether.

Acknowledgments

I would like to thank John Perazzo, who supplied indispensable research—especially for Chapter 13 on Trump's achievements—and Jim Denney, who edited the manuscript, just as he did for my previous book *Dark Agenda: The War to Destroy Christian America*. As with *Dark Agenda*, Jim helped clarify the text and make it more readable, while also providing valuable additions to support and illuminate the argument.

In addition, I want to thank Chris Ruddy, who has been a good and supportive friend throughout my career, a particularly important asset for a writer and his work. I have now written three books with Chris and Humanix that would never otherwise have seen the light of day. I am eternally grateful for that. Nor can I forget the help and support I have received from my Humanix publisher, Mary Glenn, without which all of these efforts would have been far more difficult.

Notes

PREFACE

1. https://www.politico.com/news/2020/01/22/republicans-nadler
    -cover-up-accusation-102180.
2. https://www.nbcnews.com/politics/trump-impeachment-inquiry/
    flashback-what-nadler-said-about-impeaching-president-1998
    -n1095141.
3. https://news.gallup.com/poll/284156/trump-job-approval
    -personal-best.aspx.
4. https://www.breitbart.com/politics/2020/02/11/rnc-trump
    -campaign-gop-raised-record-1m-daily-in-last-10-days-of
    -impeachment-trial/.

CHAPTER 1

1. https://www.nytimes.com/2000/11/02/us/the-2000-campaign
    -the-ad-campaign-emotional-appeal-urges-blacks-to-vote.html;
    https://townhall.com/columnists/monacharen/2005/01/07/
    dont-let-democrats-get-away-with-race-baiting-n1404714.

2. https://www.politico.com/blogs/jonathanmartin/1008/
    McCain_will_be_accused_of_racism_regardless.html; https://
    thehill.com/opinion/campaign/404543-medias-praise-for
    -mccain-is-warranted-but-where-was-it-in-08.
3. https://www.cbsnews.com/news/biden-tells-african-american
    -audience-gop-ticket-would-put-them-back-in-chains/.
4. https://www.nytimes.com/2014/10/30/us/politics/from
    -democrats-election-focus-on-racial-scars.html.
5. https://archives.frontpagemag.com/fpm/new-shame-cities
    -frontpagemagcom/.
6. Donald Trump, "Full Transcript: Donald Trump Speaks in
    https://www.politico.com/story/2016/08/donald-trump
    -michigan-speech-transcript-227221.
7. https://www.detroitnews.com/story/news/politics/2016/08/19/
    trump-chairman-resigns-ahead-mid-michigan-rally/88996014/.
8. Juan Williams, *What the Hell Do You Have to Lose?*, PublicAffairs,
    2018.
9. Ibid.
10. https://theundefeated.com/features/when-it-all-falls-down-the
    -twisted-nightmare-of-kanye-west-and-trump/.
11. https://www.realclearpolitics.com/video/2018/10/11/don_
    lemon_explodes_kanye_west_put_on_a_minstrel_show_for_
    trump_needs_a_father_figure.html.

CHAPTER 2

12. David Horowitz and Richard Poe, *The Shadow Party: How George
    Soros, Hillary Clinton, and Sixties Radicals Seized Control of the
    Democratic Party*, Thomas Nelson, 2006; David Horowitz and John
    Perazzo, *Occupy Wall Street: The Communist Movement Reborn*, The
    David Horowitz Freedom Center, 2012.
13. https://www.politico.com/story/2016/11/democrats-soros
    -trump-231313.
14. https://indivisible.org/guide.
15. https://www.realclearpolitics.com/video/2017/01/21/
    madonna_ive_thought_an_awful_lot_about_blowing_up_the_
    white_house_fuck_you.html.
16. https://news.gallup.com/poll/121391/obama-honeymoon
    -continues-months-recent-average.aspx.

17. https://www.realclearpolitics.com/articles/2017/06/27/trump_
    needed_a_honeymoon_134299.html.
18. https://prospect.org/article/2017-year-reaction-and-resistance.
19. https://www.nbcnews.com/news/us-news/civil-rights-groups
    -fight-trump-s-refugee-ban-uncertainty-continues-n713811.
20. https://www.youtube.com/watch?v=gd3fynanB5E.

CHAPTER 3

21. https://www.theguardian.com/commentisfree/2017/jul/21/
    media-war-trump-destined-fail; https://www.washingtonpost
    .com/lifestyle/style/rachel-maddow-the-lefts-powerhouse
    -on-cable-doubles-down-on-the-collusion-angle/2019/03/26/
    bd8701d0-4f36-11e9-a3f7-78b7525a8d5f_story.html.
22. Donald J. Trump and David Shiflett, *The America We Deserve*,
    Renaissance Books, 2000.
23. https://thehill.com/homenews/house/453800-cummings
    -tears-into-trump-dhs-chief-for-treatment-of-migrant-children
    -at.
24. https://www.usatoday.com/story/news/politics/2019/07/27/
    trump-lashes-out-rep-elijah-cummings-baltimore-district/
    1845890001/. (Note that Trump appears as the aggressor in this
    typical headline, when in fact the aggressor was Cummings.)
25. https://www.wbaltv.com/article/timeline-president-donald
    -trump-tweets-representative-elijah-cummings-baltimore
    -responds/28542993#.
26. https://www.breitbart.com/politics/2019/07/28/democrats
    -melt-down-over-trumps-criticism-of-cummings-disgusting
    -and-racist/.
27. Ibid.
28. Ibid.
29. Ibid.
30. https://www.breitbart.com/politics/2019/07/27/naacp-impeach
    -occupant-of-wh-for-vile-racist-attack-on-cummings/.
31. https://www.breitbart.com/the-media/2019/07/30/nolte-chris
    -matthews-compares-jews-to-rats/.
32. https://www.cnsnews.com/news/article/melanie-arter/flashback
    -rep-elijah-cummings-called-baltimore-drug-infested-20-years
    -ago.

33. https://www.newyorker.com/news/daily-comment/donald -trump-elijah-cummings-and-the-definition-of-a-rodent.

34. https://www.baltimoresun.com/opinion/editorial/bs-ed-0728 -trump-baltimore-20190727-k6ac4yvnpvcczlaexdfglifada-story .html.

35. clark.com/health-health-care/worst-cities-in-america-for-rats/.

36. J. C. Perazzo, *The New Shame of the Cities*, The David Horowitz Freedom Center, 2014..

37. https://www.frontpagemag.com/fpm/274453/shame-baltimore -frontpagemagcom.

38. https://www.biggestuscities.com/city/baltimore-maryland; https://baltimore.cbslocal.com/2019/10/25/baltimore -ranks-top-4-for-most-dangerous-cities-in-america/.

39. https://thehill.com/opinion/education/350315-baltimores -failing-schools-are-a-tragedy-of-criminal-proportions.

40. https://www.facebook.com/don.feder.9.

41. https://foxbaltimore.com/news/local/baltimore-city-gets -billions-in-federal-aid-annually; https://www.newsweek.com/ cummings-trump-baltimore-immigration-tlaib-1451411.

42. Twitter, 1:18 PM, July 28, 2019.

CHAPTER 4

43. https://www.whitehouse.gov/briefings-statements/the -inaugural-address/.

44. https://www.washingtonpost.com/politics/trump-inaugural -speech-sharp-break-with-past-and-his-party/2017/01/20/ bcfc06d6-de7a-11e6-918c-99ede3c8cafa_story.html.

45. https://slate.com/news-and-politics/2017/01/what-trump -means-when-he-talks-about-american-carnage.html.

46. https://www.npr.org/sections/itsallpolitics/2015/07/28/ 426888268/donald-trumps-flipping-political-donations.

47. Donald Trump, *The America We Deserve*, Renaissance Books, 2000.

48. https://thehill.com/homenews/administration/455210-trump -leans-into-baltimore-controversy-by-criticizing-sharpton.

49. https://www.theledger.com/opinion/20190805/bozell--graham -trump-exposes-democrat-attachment-to-sharpton.

50. Ibid.

51. https://www.mrctv.org/blog/happy-anniversary-rev-al-20-years -shapton-incited-firebombing-freddys-fashion-mart.

52. https://www.nytimes.com/2019/07/31/opinion/al-sharpton
    -trump.html?fbclid=IwAR1GWxf-rngNZbOX5rRA_8bLd_RR_
    QfXzNPt_CoYU_p0ssm0VeMARmlCifM.
53. Ibid.
54. Ibid.
55. https://www.spiked-online.com/2017/12/01/an-immigrants
    -american-dream/.
56. Jason D. Hill, *We Have Overcome: An Immigrant's Letter to the
    American People*, Bombardier Books, 2018.

CHAPTER 5

57. https://thehill.com/homenews/senate/393139-warren-on
    -family-separation-policy-trump-is-taking-america-to-a-dark
    -and-ugly.
58. Michelle Malkin, *Open Borders Inc.: Who's Funding America's
    Destruction*, Regnery Publishing, 2019.
59. Michelle Malkin, op. cit.
60. https://www.youtube.com/watch?v=CpGs5bATYbU.
61. https://en.wikipedia.org/wiki/Doublespeak.
62. David Horowitz, *Unholy Alliance: Radical Islam and the American Left*,
    Regnery Publishing, 2004.
63. https://www.aclu.org/other/draft-resolution.
64. Ibid. Police departments are to "refrain, whether acting alone or
    with federal or state law enforcement officers, from collecting
    or maintaining information about the political, religious or
    social views, associations or activities of any individual, group,
    association, organization, corporation, business or partnership
    unless such information directly relates to an investigation of
    criminal activities, and there are reasonable grounds to suspect
    the subject of the information is or may be involved in criminal
    conduct."
65. https://www.latimes.com/politics/la-pol-ca-brown-california
    -sanctuary-state-bill-20171005-story.html.
66. https://www.fairus.org/press-releases/new-fair-study-illegal
    -immigration-costs-116-billion-annually; https://
    www.businessinsider.com/california-budget-health-insurance
    -for-undocumented-residents-2019-6.
67. https://twitter.com/realdonaldtrump/status/114441941072924
    2625.

68. https://cis.org/Camarota/NonCitizens-Committed
-Disproportionate-Share-Federal-Crimes-201116.

69. Ibid.

70. https://en.wikipedia.org/wiki/2019_El_Paso_shooting.

71. https://www.buzzfeednews.com/article/briannasacks/
ice-detention-attack-killed-washington-antifa-manifesto.

72. https://www.washingtonpost.com/politics/how-do-you-stop
-these-people-trumps-anti-immigrant-rhetoric-looms-over-el
-paso-massacre/2019/08/04/62d0435a-b6ce-11e9-a091
-6a96e67d9cce_story.html?noredirect=on.

73. https://www.breitbart.com/the-media/2019/08/09/echo
-chamber-nyt-wapo-print-11-similar-talking-points-on-same-day
-to-blame-trump-for-el-paso-terror/.

74. https://thehill.com/homenews/campaign/456973-harris-on-el
-paso-shooting-trump-didnt-pull-the-trigger-but-has-been.

75. https://www.cnn.com/2019/08/03/politics/beto-orourke-el
-paso-donald-trump-racist-violence/index.html; https://thehill
.com/homenews/campaign/456078-orourke-trump-is-a-racist
-responsible-for-el-paso-shooting.

76. https://www.nbcnews.com/politics/politics-news/beto-o-rourke
-says-trump-blame-el-paso-shooting-because-n1039071.

77. https://www.rev.com/blog/donald-trump-statement-on-mass
-shootings-full-transcript-of-remarks.

78. Ibid.

79. Ibid.

80. https://www.newsweek.com/alexandria-ocasio-cortez-nyt-front
-page-trump-white-supremacy-1452724.

81. https://www.washingtonpost.com/nation/2019/08/06/new
-york-times-headline-trump-backlash/.

82. https://www.frontpagemag.com/fpm/274610/progressives
-trump-jew-among-american-politicians-bruce-thornton.

CHAPTER 6

83. https://www.breitbart.com/politics/2019/08/09/jerry-nadler
-on-his-investigation-this-is-formal-impeachment-proceedings/.

84. https://nypost.com/2001/01/23/nadler-behind-lethal-heist
-pardon/.

85. https://www.washingtonpost.com/politics/im-not-for
-impeachment-pelosi-says-potentially-roiling-fellow-democrats/

2019/03/11/894b3f80-442d-11e9-90f0-0ccfeec87a61_story
.html.

86. Andrew McCarthy, *Ball of Collusion*, Encounter Books, 2019; Greg
    Jarrett, *The Russia Hoax*, Broadside Books, 2019.

87. https://www.bustle.com/p/is-robert-mueller-a-democrat
    -republican-his-appointment-was-lauded-by-both-parties-58693.

88. https://www.realclearpolitics.com/video/2019/05/09/trump_
    mueller_in_love_with_comey.html.

89. https://www.youtube.com/watch?v=U9gmDUPdprs; at about
    the 5:30 mark, Congressman (and 2020 Democratic presidential
    hopeful) Eric Swalwell asserts without evidence that Trump is
    a "Russian agent" who is "working on behalf of the Russians."
    Examples of the daily barrage of similar baseless accusations are
    endless.

90. https://legalinsurrection.com/2017/04/fevered-swamps
    -lawrence-odonnell-promotes-bizarre-xtrump-putin-assad
    -conspiracy-theory/.

91. https://www.businessinsider.com/evidence-in-mueller-probe-in
    -the-thousands-if-not-millions-2019-3.

92. https://www.cnn.com/2019/07/21/politics/mueller
    -investigation-nadler-says-evidence-trump-guilty-high-crimes
    -misdemeanors/index.html.

93. https://www.politico.com/story/2019/08/16/house-democrats
    -intel-impeachment-1463467.

94. https://www.businessinsider.com/25th-amendment-how-can
    -you-remove-president-from-office-2017-3.

95. https://www.nationalreview.com/2016/09/hillary-clinton
    -obstruction-of-justice-email-server-deletion-was-crime/.

96. https://www.cnn.com/2019/07/17/politics/al-green
    -impeachment-resolution-text/index.html.

97. https://www.foxnews.com/media/al-green-trump-impeachment
    -public-turn-on-democrats.

98. David Horowitz and Ben Johnson, *Party of Defeat: How Democrats
    and Radicals Undermined America's War on Terror, Before and After
    9/11*, Richard Vigilante Books, 2008.

99. https://www.outsidethebeltway.com/kerry_on_iraq_wrong_
    war_wrong_place_wrong_time/.

100. https://freebeacon.com/politics/swalwell-trump-russian-agent
     -working-behalf-russians/.

CHAPTER 7

101. For a transcript of the meeting see here: https://www.breitbart
     .com/the-media/2019/08/16/nolte-new-york-times-admits-we
     -built-our-newsroom-around-russia-collusion-hoax/.
102. http://totalconservative.com/trump-slams-ny-times-for
     -embarking-on-racism-witch-hunt/.
103. Breitbart, op. cit.
104. https://www.theatlantic.com/politics/archive/2017/01/trump
     -america-first/514037/; https://www.npr.org/tags/126220956/
     america-first.
105. https://www.theguardian.com/books/2018/apr/21/end-of
     -the-american-dream-the-dark-history-of-america-first.
106. https://amgreatness.com/2019/08/16/the-mountebank-left
     -is-banking-on-you/.
107. http://www.startribune.com/the-new-york-times-1619-project
     -revisited/565907662/.
108. https://www.nytimes.com/interactive/2019/08/14/magazine/
     1619-america-slavery.html.
109. https://en.wikipedia.org/wiki/Americas#Etymology_and_
     naming.
110. https://www.loc.gov/exhibits/african-american-odyssey/free
     -blacks-in-the-antebellum-period.html.
111. https://www.smithsonianmag.com/smithsonian-institution/
     how-native-american-slaveholders-complicate-trail-tears
     -narrative-180968339/.
112. https://www.wsj.com/articles/a-look-at-african-american
     -history-through-the-numbers-11550232000.
113. http://totalconservative.com/unhinged-harvard-professor
     -trump-wants-to-reverse-outcome-of-the-civil-war/.
114. https://www.theguardian.com/global/video/2019/jul/09/nancy
     -pelosi-says-trump-wants-to-make-america-white-again-video.
115. https://www.politico.com/magazine/story/2019/07/18/
     donald-trump-racist-rally-227408.
116. https://thehill.com/homenews/house/453007-pressley
     -democrats-need-any-more-black-voices-that-dont-want-to-be-a
     -black.
117 https://thehill.com/homenews/house/453733-john-kerry
     -pressleys-story-more-american-than-any-mantle-this-president
     -could.

118. https://history.hanover.edu/courses/excerpts/111federalist.html.
119. https://www.nytimes.com/2019/03/18/us/politics/elizabeth
-warren-town-hall-electoral-college.html.
120. https://www.nbcnews.com/politics/2020-election/senate
-dems-introduce-constitutional-amendment-abolish-electoral
-college-n989656.
121. https://www.frontpagemag.com/fpm/273950/future-you-dont
-want-david-horowitz.
122. https://www.realclearpolitics.com/video/2019/08/21/
alexandria_ocasio-cortez_the_electoral_college_a_scam_has_
a_racial_injustice_breakdown.html.

CHAPTER 8

123. https://www.realclearpolitics.com/video/2019/01/05/pelosi_
on_tlaibs_motherfcker_comment_im_not_in_the_censorship_
business.html.
124. https://www.discoverthenetworks.org/individuals/rashida
-tlaib/.
125. https://www.nytimes.com/1995/01/03/obituaries/somalia-s
-overthrown-dictator-mohammed-siad-barre-is-dead.html.
126. https://www.discoverthenetworks.org/individuals/ilhan-omar/.
127. Ibid.
128. https://nypost.com/2019/07/25/ilhan-omar-suggests-people
-should-be-more-fearful-of-white-men-than-jihadists-in-2018
-interview/.
129. https://ucr.fbi.gov/crime-in-the-u.s/2018/crime-in-the-u.s.
-2018/tables/expanded-homicide-data-table-2.xls; https://ucr
.fbi.gov/crime-in-the-u.s/2018/crime-in-the-u.s.-2018/tables/
expanded-homicide-data-table-6.xls.
130. https://en.wikipedia.org/wiki/Ilhan_Omar#Israeli%E2%80%93
Palestinian_conflict.
131. https://www.usatoday.com/story/news/politics/2019/02/13/
ilhan-omar-anti-semitism-accusation-back-at-donald-trump/
2851596002/.
132 https://freebeacon.com/issues/omar-holding-secret-fundraisers
-with-islamic-groups-tied-to-terror/?fbclid=IwAR3LlYHNsQ
QdYlhRWKMEJZlTMRa2vvB1rXiFvBbNwsm0Q19h1BPbaqZ
MqO0.

133. https://www.usatoday.com/story/news/politics/2019/02/13/ ilhan-omar-anti-semitism-accusation-back-at-donald-trump/ 2851596002/.

134. https://dailycaller.com/2019/04/12/ocasio-cortez-ilhan-omar -front-page-9-11-progressive-women-color/.

135. https://www.realclearpolitics.com/video/2019/07/16/dem_rep_ tlaib_to_pelosi_acknowledge_the_fact_that_we_are_women_ of_color.html; https://www.youtube.com/watch?v=OmrfiDbQvbk.

136. https://www.foxnews.com/politics/house-passes-resolution -indirectly-calling-out-omars-anti-semitic-comments-without -mentioning-her-name.

137. https://www.realclearpolitics.com/video/2019/07/28/tlaib_bds_ about_criticizing_racist_policies_of_israel_israel_exists_to_ detriment_of_palestinians.html.

138. https://twitter.com/aipac/status/1149323328471085057? lang=en.

139. https://www.nationalreview.com/2019/08/ilhan-omar-and -rashida-tlaib-partnered-with-vicious-anti-semites-to-plan-their -trip-to-israel/.

140. https://www.politico.com/story/2019/08/19/omar-tlaib -denounce-israel-restrictions-1468985.

141. Ibid.

142. http://www.israelnationalnews.com/News/News.aspx/253558.

143. https://www.theatlantic.com/ideas/archive/2019/08/trump -assumes-disloyalty-jews/596533/.

144. https://www.tabletmag.com/jewish-news-and-politics/289871/ democratic-party-becoming-unsalvageable.

145. https://twitter.com/realdonaldtrump/status/115331587547 6463616.

CHAPTER 9

146. David Horowitz and Jacob Laksin, *The New Leviathan: How the Left-Wing Money Machine Shapes American Politics and Threatens America's Future*, Crown Forum, 2012.

147. https://www.insidesources.com/big-name-2020-dems-support -the-green-new-deal-but-big-name-enviro-groups-dont/.

148. https://www.washingtonpost.com/news/magazine/wp/2019/ 07/10/feature/how-saikat-chakrabarti-became-aocs-chief-of -change/.

149. https://www.heritage.org/energy-economics/report/assessing
-the-costs-and-benefits-the-green-new-deals-energy-policies.

150. https://www.npr.org/2019/02/07/691997301/rep
-alexandria-ocasio-cortez-releases-green-new-deal-outline.

151. https://thehill.com/policy/energy-environment/426353-ocasio
-cortez-the-world-will-end-in-12-years-if-we-dont-address;
https://www.cnbc.com/2019/02/07/aoc-just-updated-her
-massive-green-new-deal--heres-whats-in-it.html.

152. https://www.heritage.org/environment/commentary/the-green
-new-deal-would-cost-trillions-and-make-not-dimes-worth
-difference; https://www.detroitnews.com/story/opinion/2019/
01/08/ocasio-cortezs-green-new-deal-not-global-warming/
2501171002/.

153. https://www.salon.com/2019/02/07/green-dream-or-whatever
-nancy-pelosi-dismisses-alexandria-ocasio-cortezs-new-deal
-climate-plan/.

154. https://www.newsweek.com/nancy-pelosi-ocasio-cortez-green
-new-deal-broad-1347079.

155. https://www.atr.org/here-s-every-democrat-who-supports-ocasio
-cortez-s-crazy-green-new-deal.

156. https://twitter.com/ewarren/status/1170070887887986690?
lang=en.

157. C. S. Lewis, *God in the Dock*, Eerdmans, 1970.

158. https://www.washingtontimes.com/news/2019/feb/8/cory
-booker-embracing-green-new-deal-is-bold-like-/.

159. https://thehill.com/homenews/administration/429226-white
-house-blasts-aocs-green-new-deal-central-planning-disaster.

CHAPTER 10

160. David Horowitz, *Dark Agenda: The War to Destroy Christian America*,
Humanix Books, 2019.

161. https://www.courier-journal.com/story/news/2019/03/29/anti
-lgbt-comments-university-of-louisville-professor-sues-over
-demotion/3300002002/.

162. https://en.wikipedia.org/wiki/Equality_Act_(United_States)
#Support.

163. https://www.usatoday.com/story/entertainment/celebrities/
2019/08/27/trump-white-house-responds-taylor-swifts-equality
-act-petition/2135744001/.

164. https://www.heritage.org/gender/heritage-explains/the-equality
     -act.
165. Ibid.
166. Ibid.
167. https://abcnews.go.com/US/baker-won-supreme-court-case
     -maintains-cake-couple/story?id=55660012.
168. http://www.adfmedia.org/files/MasterpieceHearingTranscript
     .pdf.
169. https://abcnews.go.com/US/baker-won-supreme-court-case
     -maintains-cake-couple/story?id=55660012.
170. https://www.hrc.org/timelines/trump.
171. https://www.washingtonpost.com/outlook/five-myths/five
     -myths-about-mike-pence/2019/10/11/5f8adb6c-e9f8-11e9
     -9306-47cb0324fd44_story.html.
172. https://www.washingtontimes.com/news/2019/may/17/
     donald-trump-praises-pete-buttigieg-campaigning-wi/.
173. Ibid.

CHAPTER 11

174. https://en.wikipedia.org/wiki/Trump_derangement_syndrome.
175. https://www.washingtonpost.com/opinions/liberals-have-to
     -avoid-trump-derangement-syndrome/2017/04/13/81ff4a7a
     -2083-11e7-a0a7-8b2a45e3dc84_story.html.
176. Michiko Kakutani, *The Death of Truth: Notes on Falsehood in the Age
     of Trump*, Crown, 2018.
177. Ibid.
178. Ibid.
179. Ibid.
180. Ibid.
181. Ibid.
182. Ibid.
183. Ibid.
184. https://www.politifact.com/truth-o-meter/promises/
     trumpometer/rulings/promise-kept/.
185. https://www.breitbart.com/the-media/2019/08/16/nolte-new
     -york-times-admits-we-built-our-newsroom-around-russia
     -collusion-hoax/.
186. https://www.newyorker.com/news/daily-comment/trump
     -clarification-syndrome.

187. David Horowitz and Ben Johnson, *Party of Defeat: How Democrats and Radicals Undermined America's War on Terror Before and After 9/11*, Richard Vigilante Books, 2008.

188. https://www.youtube.com/watch?v=lzlxrPC_E_U; online video transcribed by the author.

189. https://time.com/3923128/donald-trump-announcement-speech/.

190. https://thehill.com/media/458645-cnns-chris-cuomo-trumps-mouth-is-a-threat-to-this-country.

191. https://www.heritage.org/immigration/commentary/birthright-citizenship-fundamental-misunderstanding-the-14th-amendment.

192. https://www.heritage.org/immigration/commentary/daca-unconstitutional-obama-admitted.

193. https://www.washingtonexaminer.com/weekly-standard/al-qaeda-wasnt-on-the-run.

194. https://www.realclearpolitics.com/video/2012/09/25/obama_the_future_must_not_belong_to_those_who_slander_the_prophet_of_islam.html.

CHAPTER 12

195. https://thehill.com/opinion/campaign/462658-lets-get-real-democrats-were-first-to-enlist-ukraine-in-us-elections.

196. https://www.washingtonpost.com/powerpost/pelosi-top-democrats-privately-discuss-creation-of-select-committee-for-impeachment/2019/09/24/af6f735a-dedf-11e9-b199-f638bf2c340f_story.html.

197. https://www.dailywire.com/news/watch-pelosi-slams-ukraine-call-after-admitting-she-hasnt-read-transcript.

198. https://www.nationalreview.com/news/adam-schiff-told-msnbc-we-have-not-spoken-directly-with-the-whistleblower-after-intel-aide-did-just-that/.

199. https://www.realclearinvestigations.com/articles/2019/10/30/whistleblower_exposed_close_to_biden_brennan_dnc_oppo_researcher_120996.html.

200. https://www.washingtonian.com/2019/09/24/meet-the-attorneys-representing-the-whistleblower-who-helped-launch-the-impeachment-inquiry/.

201. https://www.foxnews.com/politics/coup-has-started
     -whistleblowers-attorney-said-in-2017-posts-calling-for
     -impeachment.
202. https://thefederalist.com/2019/09/30/intel-ig-admits-it-secretly
     -erased-first-hand-information-requirement-in-august/; https://
     thefederalist.com/2019/10/07/intel-community-ig
     -stonewalling-congress-on-backdated-whistleblower-rule
     -changes/.
203. https://w ww.breitbart.com/politics/2019/11/17/emails-open
     -society-kept-alleged-whistleblower-eric-ciaramella-updated-on
     -george-soross-personal-ukraine-activities/.
204. https://www.usatoday.com/story/news/politics/2019/09/25/
     trump-releases-transcript-call-ukraine-president/2438300001/.
205. https://www.wsj.com/video/opinion-joe-biden-forced-ukraine
     -to-fire-prosecutor-for-aid-money/C1C51BB8-3988-4070-869F
     -CAD3CA0E81D8.html.
206. https://www.msn.com/en-us/news/factcheck/schiffs-parody
     -and-trumps-response/ar-AAI7Qtl.
207. https://www.nationalreview.com/news/trump-suggests-schiffs
     -parody-of-transcript-could-warrant-arrest-for-treason/.
208. https://www.docdroid.net/gt8IXKy/pac-letter-10-08-2019.pdf.
209. https://www.politico.com/news/2019/11/06/trump-louisiana
     -rally-067209.
210. https://www.breitbart.com/politics/2019/10/06/exclusive
     -stephen-miller-exposes-the-deep-state-a-collection-of
     -permanent-bureaucrats-enmeshed-inside-the-federal
     -government/.
211. Ibid.
212. Ibid.
213. https://taibbi.substack.com/p/were-in-a-permanent-coup.

CHAPTER 13
214. https://www.washingtonexaminer.com/washington-secrets/
     trumps-list-289-accomplishments-in-just-20-months-relentless
     -promise-keeping.
215. https://www.nato.int/nato_static_fl2014/assets/pdf/pdf_
     2019_06/20190625_PR2019-069-EN.pdf.
216. https://www.theguardian.com/world/2009/mar/25/obama
     -war-terror-overseas-contingency-operations.

217. https://www.foxnews.com/politics/trump-national-security
-strategy-restores-reference-to-jihadist-terror-threat.

218. https://www.foxnews.com/opinion/obamas-team-had-the
-chance-to-kill-isis-leader-al-baghdadi-and-they-blew-it.

219. https://heavy.com/news/2019/10/abu-bakr-al-baghdadi/.

220. https://www.breitbart.com/clips/2019/10/29/biden-isis-leader
-killed-in-spite-of-trumps-actions/.

221. https://www.washingtontimes.com/news/2017/jul/5/current
-time-broadcasts-into-russia-eastern-europe/.

222. https://www.politico.eu/article/donald-trump-crackdown-on
-rights-abusers-in-russia/.

223. https://www.washingtonexaminer.com/steve-mnuchin-no
-russia-sanctions-waiver-for-exxon-other-companies.

224. https://www.bbc.com/news/world-us-canada-39487617.

225. https://www.rferl.org/a/un-us-leaves-unesco-anti-israel-bias/
28789963.html.

226. https://www.timesofisrael.com/us-state-department-withholds
-additional-45-million-from-unrwa/.

227. https://www.wsj.com/articles/u-s-will-cut-millions-in-funding
-to-u-n-palestinian-agency-1535739845.

228. https://www.wsj.com/articles/u-s-to-cut-over-200-million-in
-palestinian-aid-1535145774.

229. https://thehill.com/homenews/administration/405873-stat
e-department-announces-closure-of-plo-mission-in-washington.

230. https://thehill.com/homenews/administration/435628-trump
-announces-us-recognition-of-israeli-claim-on-golan-heights.

231. https://www.timesofisrael.com/trumps-state-department-no
-longer-calls-west-bank-occupied-in-annual-report/.

232. https://www.frontpagemag.com/fpm/2019/11/legality
-jewish-settlements-judea-and-samaria-joseph-puder/.

233. https://nypost.com/2018/05/23/trump-lambastes-ms-13-refers
-to-them-as-animals-again/.

234. https://www.cnbc.com/2019/10/08/nearly-1-million-migrants
-arrested-along-the-southern-border-in-fiscal-2019.htm.

235. https://www.foxnews.com/politics/trump-travel-ban-30000
-people-blocked-muslim-state-department.

236. https://www.snopes.com/fact-check/trump-parade-1995/.

237. https://www.breitbart.com/politics/2019/11/11/donald-trump
-has-fired-demoted-or-suspended-over-8000-veterans-affairs
-employees-since-taking-office/.

238. https://www.military.com/daily-news/2019/07/30/veterans-win -trump-administrations-mission-act-reforms.html.

239. https://www.breitbart.com/politics/2019/11/11/donald-trump -has-fired-demoted-or-suspended-over-8000-veterans-affairs -employees-since-taking-office/.

240. https://thehill.com/blogs/blog-briefing-room/news/281936 -obama-to-trump-what-magic-wand-do-you-have.

241. https://www.forbes.com/sites/chuckdevore/2019/07/10/in -trumps-first-30-months-manufacturing-up-by-314000-jobs -over-obama-what-states-are-hot/#4411d1712677; https:// www.marketwatch.com/story/manufacturing-employment-in -the-us-is-at-the-same-level-of-69-years-ago-2019-01-04.

242. https://www.nytimes.com/2019/11/04/climate/trump-paris -agreement-climate.html; https://ballotpedia.org/Fact_check/ China,_India,_and_the_Paris_Climate_Agreement.

243. https://www.washingtonexaminer.com/washington-secrets/ trumps-list-289-accomplishments-in-just-20-months-relentless -promise-keeping.

244. https://www.nytimes.com/2018/01/04/climate/trump-offshore -drilling.html; https://www.washingtonexaminer.com/ washington-secrets/trumps-list-289-accomplishments-in-just -20-months-relentless-promise-keeping.

245. https://thehill.com/blogs/blog-briefing-room/news/281936 -obama-to-trump-what-magic-wand-do-you-have.

246. https://www.cnbc.com/2019/09/11/minorities-ages-25-to -54-make-up-most-new-hires-in-workforce.html; https:// www.census.gov/library/publications/2019/demo/p60-266 .html.

247. https://www.dailysignal.com/2019/09/09/over-6-million -americans-drop-off-food-stamps-since-trump-took-office/.

248. https://www.cmegroup.com/education/articles-and-reports/ russell-us-equity-indices-2019-reconstitution-results.html.

249. https://www.wsj.com/articles/trumps-middle-class-economic -progress-11569786435.

250. David Horowitz, *Dark Agenda: The War to Destroy Christian America,* Humanix Books, 2019.

251. https://www.nbcnews.com/politics/national-security/trump -administration-launches-global-effort-end-criminalization -homosexuality-n973081.

252. https://www.theguardian.com/us-news/2017/apr/28/donald -trump-nra.

253. https://www.realclearpolitics.com/video/2018/12/19/van_ jones_prison_reform_bill_a_christmas_miracle.html.

254. https://www.foxnews.com/opinion/deroy-murdock-media -trump-outreach-minorities.

255. https://www.whitehouse.gov/briefings-statements/remarks -president-trump-2019-national-historically-black-colleges -universities-week-conference/.

CHAPTER 14

256. Donald Trump, *The America We Deserve*, Renaissance Books, 2000.

257. Ibid.

258. https://www.realclearpolitics.com/video/2019/02/05/trump_ america_will_never_be_a_socialist_country_we_were_born_ free_and_we_shall_stay_free.html.

259. https://www.conservapedia.com/Long_march_through_the_ institutions.

260. David Horowitz and Jacob Laksin, *The New Leviathan: How the Left-Wing Money Machine Shapes American Politics and Threatens America's Future*, Crown Forum, 2012; https://en.wikipedia.org/wiki/The_ long_march_through_the_institutions; for the Soros organized and funded power base of the open borders left, see Michelle Malkin, *Open Borders Inc.: Who's Funding America's Destruction*, Regnery Publishing, 2019.

261. https://www.realclearpolitics.com/video/2019/08/09/kamala_ harris_no_longer_a_debatable_point_that_trump_is_a_white_ supremacist_possesses_hate.html.

262. https://freebeacon.com/politics/buttigieg-if-you-support -trumps-immigration-policies-you-support-racism/.

263. https://www.brookings.edu/blog/fixgov/2019/08/14/trump -and-racism-what-do-the-data-say/.

264. https://www.breitbart.com/clips/2019/08/25/psychiatrist-on -cnn-trump-may-be-responsible-for-millions-of-more-deaths -than-hitler-stalin-mao/.

265. https://www.azquotes.com/quote/1137804.

266. https://www.motherjones.com/politics/2019/09/kamala-harris -delivers-a-message-to-donald-trump-theres-one-reason-you -havent-been-indicted/.

267. https://www.newsweek.com/beto-orourke-trump-white
     -supremacist-mortal-danger-people-color-2020-debate-1459088.
268. https://twitter.com/rashidatlaib/status/1170423606087692289?
     lang=en.
269. https://www.buzzfeednews.com/article/rubycramer/elizabeth
     -warren-debate-2020-primary; https://reason.com/2019/08/12/
     warren-wants-big-structural-change-that-goes-beyond-anything
     -previous-democratic-administrations-have-proposed/.
270. https://theintercept.com/2019/12/12/the-inspector
     -generals-report-on-2016-fb-i-spying-reveals-a-scandal-of
     -historic-magnitude-not-only-for-the-fbi-but-also-the-u-s
     -media/?menu=1.

Index

Abortion, 181
"Abuse of power" charge, ix, 201
Africa, slavery in, 78–80, 195
African Americans
    benefits of Trump's policies for,
        80–82, 182–183
    as Democratic supporters, 7–9
    in identity politics, 46
    political correctness for, 29–31,
        40
    racism by, 36, 40, 42, 44–45,
        83–84
    and slavery, 77–81, 195
    Trump's treatment of, 8–10
    West–Trump meeting at White
        House, 11–12
Agriculture Department, 179
Alice in Wonderland (Carroll), 66
Al Jazeera, 92–93
Al-Qaeda, 55, 92, 141

Al-Shabab, 92
America First Committee, 75
"America First" slogan, 17, 71, 75,
    76, 80, 182
"American carnage" speech, 38–40
American Civil Liberties Union
    (ACLU), 51, 52, 117
"American Come Home" slogan, 70
American Dream, 112, 183–184,
    186–187
American Israel Pac (AIPAC), 94
The America We Deserve (Trump), 27,
    37, 40, 186
Anchor babies, 80–81
Antifa, 54, 55
Anti-Semitism, 43, 93–96, 99, 101,
    133, 134
Arabs, in Israel, 97–98, 101, 172, 173
Arevalo-Carranza, Carlos, 47
Arizona, 3

Ashrawi, Hanan, 99, 101
Assad, Bashar al-, 24, 65, 167
"Assailing Hate But Not Guns," 58
Asylum seekers, 49
Athens, ancient, 15
Atkinson, Michael, 148
Automobiles, in Green New Deal, 106, 110–111, 204, 211

Baghdadi, Abu Bakr al-, 169
Bakaj, Andrew, 148
Baltimore, Maryland, 7, 30–36, 40, 41, 207
Baltimore Sun, 33–34
Bannon, Steve, 75
Baquet, Dean, 73–76, 130
Barr, William, 143, 146, 154
Barre, Siad, 92
Behold, America (Churchwell), 76
Benghazi terrorist attack, 141
Beria, Lavrenti, 159, 192
Betts, Connor Stephen, 54
Biden, Hunter, 145, 152, 153
Biden, Joe, 6, 30–31, 44, 144–146, 148, 151–153, 170
Bigotry, resolution to condemn, 96
Birthright citizenship, 139–140
Black Lives Matter, 14, 91
"Blame America First" convention (1984), 205–206
Blumenthal, Richard, 16
Booker, Cory, 11, 16, 56, 96, 111, 208
Border security, 20–21, 28, 49, 137, 173–174
Boston Marathon bombing (2013), 52
Bouie, Jamelle, 39
Boycott, Divest, and Sanctions (BDS) movement, 98, 99, 134
Brawley, Tawana, 42
Brazil, slavery in, 79
Brennan, John, 63, 151
British colonies, slavery in, 77–78, 195
Brookings Institute, 191

"Brown menace," 139–140
Burisma Holdings, 145
Bush, George W., 5, 70, 71, 132, 135, 168, 179
Bush Derangement Syndrome, 132–133
"Bush lied, people died" slogan, 70
Buttigieg, Pete, 56, 120, 121, 190–191, 211
Byrd, James, Jr., 5

California, 18, 52, 53, 205
Capital Financing Program, 183
Capitalism, 111–112, 197–198
Carbon emissions, 108
Carroll, Lewis, 66
Carter, Jimmy, 210
Catholic hospitals, lawsuits against, 117
Cato, Gavin, 43
CBS This Morning, 95
Central Intelligence Agency (CIA), 144, 148
Chakrabarti, Saikat, 104
Chaly, Valeriy, 146
Charen, Mona, 5
Charlottesville, Virgina, protest in, 81–82
Chemical weapons, in Syria, 124, 167
Cheney, Liz, 96
Chicago, Illinois, 7, 33, 40, 91, 207
China, 26, 108, 133, 135–136, 163–164, 177–178, 186
Chomsky, Noam, 91
Christchurch, New Zealand, mass shooting, 54
Churchwell, Sarah, 76
Ciaramella, Eric, 147–151
Cincinnati, Ohio, 7
Cipollone, Pat, 156
Citizenship, 51, 54, 79, 81, 131, 139–140, 204
Civil Rights Acts, 79, 116–117
Civil Rights Revolution, 10, 42–45, 199

Civil War, U.S., 79–81, 196, 202, 209

Clark, William, 82

Climate change, 104, 105, 107, 108, 111

Clinton, Bill, and administration, x–xi, 61, 120, 135, 182

Clinton, Hillary, xi, 1–4, 27, 63, 64, 68, 83, 85, 144, 146, 190, 210

CNN, 25, 64, 131, 140, 196

Coal industry, 177

Cold Civil War, 185–202, 209
  and 2020 reelection campaign, 199–200
  Democratic attacks in, 190–191
  Democrats' hatred of Trump, 187–189
  impeachment proceedings in, 201–202
  O'Rourke in, 194–197
  search for impeachable offense in, 192–194
  and Trump's political ambition, 185–187
  Warren in, 197–199

Cold War, 69–70, 94, 109, 199

Collman, Diane, 47–48

Colorado, 85

Colorado Civil Rights Commission, 118, 119

Comey, James, 63, 64, 144

Command economy, 104, 109

Communism, 107, 108–110, 211. *See also* Government-run health care; Green New Deal

Confederate monuments, removal of, 81–82

Congressional obstruction, 48, 128, 203

Connecticut, 2

Constitution, U.S., x, xi, 15, 67, 85–86, 90, 156, 208–209

Corporate tax rate, 178

Council on American Islamic Relations (CAIR), 91, 95

Crime(s)
  committed by illegal aliens, 53

high crimes and misdemeanors, 65–66
  impeachable, 67–69, 192–194
  violent, 7, 34, 38, 41, 138, 173–174, 205

Crown Heights, Brooklyn, riots in, 43, 44

Crusius, Patrick, 53–54

Cummings, Elijah, 29–37, 40, 41, 45, 46, 208

Cuomo, Chris, 138–140

Current Time (network), 170

Dakota Access Pipeline, 178

Daniels, "Stormy," 67

Dayton, Ohio, mass shooting in, 54–59

Dean, Howard, 132–133

The Death of Truth (Kakutani), 124–131

De Blasio, Bill, 44

Declaration of Independence, 90, 209

Deep state, 67, 143–159
  and administration's cooperation with investigation, 156
  Ciaramella's whistleblower complaint, 147–150
  and firing of Comey, 63
  impeachment attempt as legislative coup, 157–159
  Miller on, 157–158
  sabotage of Trump presidency by, 28, 200
  Trump's phone call with Zelensky, 151–155
  and Ukrainian intervention in U.S. elections, 144–147

Deere, Judd, 111, 116

Defense policy, 164–166

Deferred Action for Childhood Arrivals (DACA), 48, 141

Democracy Alliance, 13–15

Democratic National Committee (DNC), 6, 64, 144, 210

Democratic Party and members
  anti-American sentiments by,
    81–82, 194–199
  approach to politics of, xii–xiii
  boycott of Trump inauguration
    by, 16, 127
  control of inner cities by, 7–8,
    34–36
  demonization of Trump by,
    19–21, 187–189, 193–194
  illegal immigration issue for,
    48–50, 53
  in impeachment inquiry/
    proceedings, 61–62, 66, 69,
    155–156, 159
  Jewish supporters of, 100, 101
  lies told by, 207–212
  opposition to Electoral College
    by, 85–86
  partisan politics during wartime
    by, 70–71
  as "Party of No," 19–22
  racism charge against
    Republicans by, 4–11
  resistance to Trump presidency
    by, xi–xii
  response to El Paso and Dayton
    mass shootings by, 55–59
  strength and number attacks on
    Trump by, 190–191
  support for Green New Deal by,
    103–104
  support of Sharpton by, 43–46
  support of the Squad by, 90–91,
    96
  suppression of free speech by,
    115–116
  Trump's political donations to,
    40
Denmark, 133, 136–137
Department of Homeland Security,
  51, 102
Department of Veterans Affairs
  (VA), 175, 176
Deplorables, xii, 6, 17, 27, 83, 190,
  204

Deregulation policies, 24, 177–179,
  186
Dershowitz, Alan, 159
Detroit, Michigan, 7, 40
Detroit News, 9
Devine, Tad, 145
Discrimination, 116, 118–119, 186
Doublespeak, 50
"Draining the swamp," 32, 162
Drugs, illegal, 32–33, 138
Dual loyalty, 93–94, 100
Durham, John, 143, 146

Economy, 53, 105, 109, 111, 137,
  176–179
Education system. See Public
  schools
Elections and campaigns
  2000 presidential, 5
  2004 presidential, 71
  2008 presidential, 5
  2012 presidential, 6
  2016 presidential, 1–5, 15–17,
    38–40, 62–64, 71, 83, 85,
    127–130, 137, 145–146,
    151–153, 190, 193, 203, 204,
    209
  2018 congressional, 65, 89–90
  2020 presidential, 53, 67–69,
    146, 187, 199–200, 204
Electoral College, 3, 15, 84–87, 204,
  208–209
Elias, Marc, 144
Ellison, Keith, 14
El Paso mass shooting, 53–59, 62
Email scandal, Hillary Clinton's, 68
Emancipation Proclamation, 77
The Emerging Democratic Majority
  (Judis and Teixeira), 48
Energy production, 105, 204
England, 167, 195
"Equality," 113–121
  and First Amendment rights of
    religious people, 118–121
  Josephson on gender identity,
    114–115

passage of Equality Act, 115–118
and religious liberty in United
States, 113–114
Trump's support of equal
opportunities, 40–41
Equality Act (HR 1), 115–118
Erdoğan, Recep, 26
European Union, 163, 166
Evangelicals, 113
Executive *diktat,* 104, 110
Executive Order 13793, 175

Factionalism, xi, 15, 17, 84–85,
208–209
Farrakhan, Louis, 42, 91, 101
Feder, Don, 35
Federal Bureau of Investigation
(FBI), 62–64, 200
Federal government, 38, 161–162,
177
The Federalist Papers, #10 (Madison),
84, 86
The Final Call, 91
First Amendment, 114, 118–121,
180, 205, 211
First Step Act, 11, 182, 189
Fisher, Marc, 38–39
Flake, Floyd, 40
Florida, 2
Food stamp program, 179, 186
Ford, Henry, 133, 134
Foreign Intelligence Surveillance
Court (FISA court), 64, 144,
200
Foreign policy, 69–71, 137, 167,
170–173
Fourteenth Amendment, 140
Fox, Tom, 174
Fox News, 121
France, 167
Frances, Allen, 192
Frank, Thomas, 23–24
#FraudNewsCNN, 25
Freddy's Fashion Mart (Harlem),
43
Frederiksen, Mette, 136–137

Freedom, 111, 198, 199–200, 203,
209, 212. *See also* Religious
liberty
Free speech, 114–116
Fusion GPS, 144, 145

Gay, Mara, 76
Gay marriage, 121
Gender dysphoria, 114–115, 117
Gender identity, 114–115, 117
Germany, 165
Gessen, Masha, 127
Get Out of Jail Free cards, 205
Gillespie, Ed, 161
Gillibrand, Kirsten, 96
Giuliani, Rudy, 152, 154
Global Compact on Migration, 171
Globalism, 49–51, 80
Global Magnitsky Human Rights
Accountability Act, 170
Global War on Terror, 168
Golan Heights, 173
Goldman, John, 145–146
Gorsuch, Neil, 180
Government-run (single-payer) health
care, 107, 197, 205, 211, 212
Graham, Lindsey, 139
Gramsci, Antonio, 187
Grann, David, 125
Green, Al, 68–69, 194
Greenland, 133, 136
Green New Deal, 103–112, 198, 200
described, 204–205
grandiose communist ambitions
in, 108–110
lies told by Democrats about, 211
negative impact of, on United
States, 105–108
Ocasio-Cortez's announcement
of, 103–105
totalitarianism to implement,
110–112
Grenell, Richard, 121
Guantanamo Bay detention center,
168–169
Gun control, 58, 135, 181

Hamas, 91, 92, 98–101, 134, 171
Harris, Kamala, 44, 48, 51, 56, 96,
    188–189, 193–194, 208
Health care, 107, 175–176, 197, 200,
    205, 211, 212
Health insurance, 53, 110, 197
Hearsay evidence, of collusion, 150,
    151
Heritage Foundation, 114, 116–117
Hezbollah, 100, 166, 171
Hezbollah International Financing
    Prevention Amendments Act,
    169
Hill, Jason, 45–46
Hilton, Paris, 5
Hirono, Mazie, 208
Historically Black Colleges and
    Universities (HBCUs),
    183–184
Hitler, Adolf, 97, 125, 132, 192
Holocaust, 97
Homophobia, xii, 6, 83, 120–121,
    190, 204, 205
Horowitz, Michael, 200
House Foreign Affairs Committee,
    93, 95, 96, 134
Household income, 179
House Intelligence Committee,
    65–67, 148
House Judiciary Committee, 61,
    65, 67
House of Representatives, U.S., ix, x,
    108–109, 116, 147
HR 2047 bill, 101–102
Huffington Post, 23
Human rights, 188–189, 200, 212
Human Rights Campaign, 120
Hunt, Kasie, 2–3
Hussein, Saddam, 132

Identity politics, 37–46, 187
    and "American carnage"
        campaign speech, 38–40
    and conservative thought/
        expression, 205
    racism inherent in, 46, 204, 207

Sharpton's role in, 41–46
    the Squad's use of, 83–84, 86–87
    and Trump as populist, 37–38
    and Trump's support for equal
        opportunities, 40–41
"Ignore It at Your Peril" (Leibovitz),
    101
Illegal immigration, 47–59, 204, 205
    and accusations of racism
        against Trump, 190–191
    anchor babies and, 80–81
    decriminalization of, 21
    economic costs of, 53
    and mass shootings in El Paso
        and Dayton, 53–59
    murder of Bambi Larson, 47–49
    by Omar's family, 92
    and open borders policy, 20,
        49–52, 204
    and Sanctuary Cities, 51–52
    Trump's position on, 28, 131,
        137–140, 173–174
Illinois, 2
Immigrant detention centers, 20,
    29–30, 48–50, 188–190
Immigration and Customs
    Enforcement (ICE), 20, 54,
    102, 174
Immigration and Nationality Act, 92
Immigration policy, 189–191
    ban on, to prevent terrorism,
        17–19, 140, 174, 190
    and conflict over border wall,
        20–21, 49
    under Obama, 141
    slavery and, 80–81
Impeachment of Donald J. Trump,
    61–71
    administration's cooperation
        with inquiry, 156
    attacks on rhetoric in, 137
    in Cold Civil War against
        Trump, 201–202
    foreign policy impact of, 69–71
    inquiry into collusion with
        Ukraine, 146–147, 149

Intelligence Committee's
   involvement in, 65–67
as legislative coup, 157–159
and Mueller investigation, 62–65
opening of formal proceedings,
   61–62
partisan politics in, ix, x,
   208–209
as part of Resistance strategy,
   204
to prevent reelection, 67–69
search for impeachable offense
   in, 192–194
Senate's vote on, ix–x
Tlaib's remarks about, 90–91
Trump's approval ratings
   during, xii
Zaid's tweets about, 149
India, 108, 177–178
Indivisible (organization), 14
Infrastructure investment, 21–22
Ingraham, Laura, 47
Inner cities, 7, 33–41, 45–46
Inslee, Jay, 31
Inspector General of the
   Intelligence Community
   (ICIG), 147, 149, 150, 200
Intermediate-Range Nuclear Forces
   Treaty, 170
Iran, 100, 134, 139, 165–166, 171,
   186, 206, 210
Iran Nuclear Deal, 165–166, 206,
   210
Iraq, 166
Iraq and Syria Genocide Relief and
   Accountability Act, 167
Iraq War, 70–71, 132, 169
Islamic Caliphate, 24, 137, 140, 168,
   169
Islamic State of Iraq and Syria
   (ISIS), 55, 140, 168, 169
Islamic terrorism, war on, 168–170
Islamophobia, xii, 6, 92–93, 190,
   204, 205
Israel, 93–94, 96–97, 99–102, 134,
   137, 166, 171–173, 211–212

Japan, 163, 186
Japanese internment, 111
Jefferson, Thomas, 82, 209
Jeffries, Hakeem, 182
Jerusalem, 91, 172
Jews, 94, 96–98, 100, 101. *See also*
   Anti-Semitism
Jihad, 93, 168
Johnson, Alice, 189
Johnson, Jack, 10
Jones, Van, 182
Josephson, Allan, 114–115
Judis, John B., 48

Kakutani, Michiko, 124–131, 140
Kavanaugh, Brett, 180
Kerry, John, 70–71, 83, 84
Keystone XL Pipeline, 178
KGB (Committee for State
   Security), 159, 210
Khan Shaykhun, Syria, sarin attack,
   124, 167
Kim Jong-Un, 25–26
King, Gayle, 95
King, Martin Luther, Jr., 44, 45, 207
Ku Klux Klan (KKK), 16, 76, 82
Kushner, Jared, 182

LaPierre, Wayne, 133
Larson, Bambi, 47–49
Lee, Robert E., 82
Legal immigration, 50–51, 131
Leibovich, Mark, 161–162
Leibovitz, Liel, 101
Lemon, Don, 12
Lenin, Vladimir, 129
Lenin's Tomb (Remnick), 132
"Let's Get Real" (Goldman), 145–146
Lewandowski, Corey, 67
Lewis, C. S., 110
Lewis, Meriwether, 82
LGBTQ community, 116–118,
   120–121, 181, 211
Lindbergh, Charles, 75
Little Sisters of the Poor, 180
Lobbying, 161–162

LoBianco, Tom, 120–121
London Bridge, terror attack on, 25
Loury, Glenn, 43, 44

Maddow, Rachel, 24, 131
Madison, James, 84, 86
Madonna, 15, 127
Mainstream media, 23–36. *See also* Trump derangement syndrome
    attacks on Trump in, 23–24, 130–131
    charges of racism against Trump in, 32–34
    on conditions in Baltimore, 34–36
    criticism of Trump's Twitter feed by, 24–29
    El Paso mass shooting in, 55–59
    impeachment inquiry in, 192
    Mueller investigation in, 64–65
    Shayrat Airbase missile strike in, 124
    Trump–Cummings conflict in, 29–36
    Trump's presidential campaign in, 4–5
"Make America Great Again" slogan, 17, 80, 182
"Make America Safe Again" slogan, 19, 28, 53, 71
Manafort, Paul, 145, 146
Manufacturing industries, 105, 176–177
Mao Zedong, 192
March for Life, 181
Martin Luther King Day, 207
Marx, Karl, 104
Masterpiece Cakeshop (Colorado), 118–119
Matthews, Chris, 32
McAleenan, Kevin, 29
McCabe, Andrew, 67
McCain, John, 5
McCollum, Betty, 101
McGovern, George, 70

Meadows, Mark, 155
"The Meaning of 'American Carnage'"(Bouie), 39
Mein Kampf (Hitler), 97
Mexico, 137–138, 163, 186, 190
Michigan, 2, 3, 89
MIFTAH (Palestinian Initiative for the Promotion of Global Dialogue and Democracy), 99
Military funding, 105–106, 165–166
Military mobilization, in Green New Deal, 111, 200, 204, 211
Miller, Stephen, 157–158, 162
Minneapolis City Council, 92
Minnesota, 89, 90
Mohamed, Nur Omar, 92
Monroe, Louisiana, 156
Moore, Michael, 91
MSNBC, 64, 131, 148
MS-13 gang, 174
Mueller, Robert, 63–65, 67, 200, 210
Mueller Report, 61–65, 67, 131, 143, 149, 152
Mughrabi, Dalal Al, 99
Murphy, Chris, 31
Murtaugh, Tim, 149
"Muslim ban," 17–19, 140, 174, 190
Muslim Brotherhood, 91, 93, 97
Muslims, 18, 19, 89–93, 97–98

Nadler, Jerrold, x–xi, 30, 61, 65–67, 69, 90
National Action Network, 44
National anthem, athlete's protests during, 181–182
National Association for the Advancement of Colored People (NAACP), 5, 31, 182
National Museum of African American History, 77
National Rifle Association, 133, 135
Nation of Islam, 101
Navy, U.S., 170
Neo-Nazis, 82, 99
New York, New York, 7
New York State, 205

New York Times, 23, 73–77, 80, 130–132, 196, 206, 209
New Yorker, 132–137
9/11 attacks, 51, 95, 168
1984 (Orwell), 50
North America, slavery in, 79
North Atlantic Treaty Organization (NATO), 24, 137, 165
North Carolina, 2
"Not My President" slogan, xi, 15, 127
"No Trump, No Wall, No USA at all" slogan, 49
Nuclear power plants, 106

Nuclear weapons, 165, 166, 170
Obama, Barack, and administration, 5, 6, 10, 14, 16, 20, 21, 24, 25, 43, 48, 49, 68, 75, 80, 119, 124, 135, 139, 140, 144–145, 164–170, 172, 174, 175–178, 180–181, 187–189, 206, 210
Obamacare, 140
"Obstruction of Congress" charge, ix, 201
"Obstruction of justice" charge, 63, 65, 67, 68
Ocasio-Cortez, Alexandria, 56, 58, 83, 86–87, 95, 103–105, 107–108, 109, 111, 188, 211
Occupy Wall Street, 14
Odeh, Rasmea, 91
O'Donnell, Lawrence, 65, 211
Ohr, Bruce, 145
Ohr, Nellie, 145
Oil and gas industry, 106, 109, 178, 197
Omar, Ilhan, 56, 83, 89, 92–96, 98–102, 134, 188
One state solution, 96–98
Open borders policy, 20, 49–52, 204
O'Rourke, Beto, 11, 56, 194–197
Orwell, George, 50

Pagones, Steven, 42
Pakistan, 169

Palestine, 90–91, 97, 171–172, 211–212
Palestine Liberation Organization (PLO), 99, 172
Paris Climate Accord, 177–178
Patriot Act, 51
Patriotism, 17, 75–76, 80, 162, 181–182, 199
Pelosi, Nancy, 14, 21, 30, 62, 81, 91, 93–95, 108–109, 146–149, 156, 201, 208–209
Pence, Karen, 121
Pence, Mike, 96, 119–121
Pennsylvania, 2, 3
Perkins Coie, 144
Perry, Katy, 2, 3
Phillips, Jack, 118–119, 181
Podesta, John, 3
Podesta, Tony, 145
Police departments, 51–52
Political correctness, 4, 6, 25, 27–29, 32, 33, 40
PolitiFact website, 129, 130
Pompeo, Mike, 143
Popular Front for the Liberation of Palestine, 91
Popular vote, in 2016 election, 14, 85–86
Populism, xiii, 17, 37–38
Poroshenko, Petro, 146
Poverty, 7, 32, 38, 179
Presidential honeymoon period, 16–17
Pressley, Ayanna, 56, 83–84, 95
Prison reform, 11, 182, 189
Private health insurance, 110, 197
Profits, over people, 197–198
Progressives
    "American carnage" and social policy of, 39
    anti-American sentiments of, 75–76
    and bluntness of Trump's tweets, 28
    Green New Deal for, 103, 104

Progressives (*continued*)
  rejection of American Dream by,
    186–187
  suppression of free speech and
    religious liberty by, 114, 116,
    121
  The 1619 Project for, 80
  Trump presidency for, 4–5
  use of political correctness by,
    31–32, 36
  views of inner cities by, 45–46
Protestant Christians, 113
Public schools, 7, 34, 38, 40–41, 197
Pueblo Sin Fronteras (Village
    Without Borders), 50
Pulitzer Center, 77, 196, 209
Putin, Vladimir, 24, 26, 64–65, 69,
    71, 127, 130–131, 170

Quid pro quo, 154
Quinn, Jack, 161, 162
Quinn Gillespie & Associates, 161
Qur'an, 90

Racial minorities, 48, 75, 93,
    179, 208. *See also* African
    Americans
Racism, 73–87
  accusations of, against
    Republicans, 4–11, 207–208
  accusations of, against Trump,
    4, 6–10, 14, 15, 19, 30–33,
    37, 44, 56–57, 81, 83, 183,
    188–191, 194–195
  of black politicians, 36, 40, 42,
    44–45, 83–84
  and identity politics, 46, 204, 207
  and opposition to Electoral
    College, 84–87
  as part of American heritage, 10,
    195, 209
  and patriotism, 75–76
  and slavery in United States,
    79–81
  Squad's use of, 93, 95, 96, 98,
    101–102

and "The 1619 Project," 76–79
  and tribalism by anti-American
    left, 81–84
  at Unite the Right rally, 82
  and views of illegal immigration,
    50
  white, 73–75
Ramos, Jorge, 190
Reagan, Ronald, 207
Religious Freedom Restoration Act,
    120
Religious liberty, 113–114, 116–121,
    180, 205, 211
Remnick, David, 132–137, 140
Republican Guard, of Iran, 100
Republican Party and members
  accusations of racism against,
    4–11, 207–208
  approach to politics of, xii–xiii
  approval ratings for, during
    Trump impeachment, xi
  lies told by Democrats about,
    207–209
  response to El Paso and Dayton
    mass shootings by, 55
  response to Omar's anti-Semitic
    comments by, 96
Resistance strategy, 13–22, 203–204
  in Cold Civil War, 201–202,
    209
  Democracy Alliance meeting
    creating, 13–15
  and Democrats as "Party of No,"
    19–22
  illegal immigration in, 49, 50
  impeachment as goal of, 62, 69
  institutions of society in, 187
  and legitimacy of Trump's
    election, xi, 15–17, 127
  and "Muslim ban," 17–19
  slander in, 82
Revolutionary War (American
    Revolution), 78–79
Rice, Susan, 151
Rights coalition, 187
Romney, Mitt, 6

Roosevelt, Franklin D., and administration, 111
Rosenbaum, Yankel, 43
Rosenberg, Susan, 61
Rosenstein, Rod, 63, 67
Russia
    Democratic collusion with, 34, 144, 146
    policy toward, 69, 167, 170–171
    Trump's alleged collusion with, 24, 62–63, 73–74, 130, 131, 201, 203, 206, 210–211
Ryan, Paul, 6, 31, 63–64

St. Louis, Missouri, 7, 207
Sanctuary Cities movement, 51–52, 204, 205
Sanders, Bernie, 55, 96, 104, 183, 197, 211
Sarsour, Linda, 15, 91, 101
Scalia, Antonin, 180
Scalise, Steve, 55, 96
Schiff, Adam, 65, 66, 147, 148, 151, 153–155
School choice, 40–41
Schumer, Chuck, 63
Second Amendment, 181
Senate, U.S., ix–x, 85, 116, 166, 210
September 11 terrorist attacks, 51, 95, 168
Sessions, Jeff, 16
Sexism, xii, 6, 15, 83, 190, 204, 205
Sharpton, Al, 41–46
Shayrat Airbase, Syria, cruise missile strike, 123–124, 167
Single-payer (government-run) health care, 107, 197, 205, 211, 212
"The 1619 Project," 76–79, 130, 196, 206, 209
Slavery, 77–81, 195–196, 206, 209
Socialism, 104–106, 109, 187, 198, 204–205, 211
Somalia, 92
Soros, George, 13, 15, 20, 49, 50, 103, 127, 151, 203

South Bend, Indiana, 120
South China Sea, 164
Space Force, 165
Spears, Britney, 5
Speier, Jackie, 67
Sperry, Paul, 148
Spicer, Sean, 127
The Squad, 56, 89–102
    2018 election of, 89–90
    anti-Semitic comments by, 93–96
    and identity politics, 83–84, 86–87
    impeachment remarks by, 90–91
    link to terrorist organizations, 92–93
    response to criticism of, 95–96
    support of one state solution by, 96–98
    West Bank trip by, 99–102
Stalin, Josef, 125, 159, 192
State Department, 174
State of the Union Address (2019), 187
Steele, Christopher, 63, 64, 144, 146, 200, 210
Stelter, Brian, 192
Strzok, Peter, 63
Supreme Court, 118–119, 180, 181
Swalwell, Eric, 71, 210–211
Syria, 167, 173

Taibbi, Matt, 158–159
Taiwan, 164
Tapper, Jake, 98
Tariffs, 163–164
Taxes and tax policy, 24, 178, 211
Teixeira, Ruy, 48
Tennessee, 2
Terrorism, 17–19, 91–94, 99, 100, 140, 168–170, 174, 190
This Town (Leibovich), 161–162
Tlaib, Rashida, 56, 83, 89–91, 95–102, 134, 197
Totalitarianism, 105, 107, 110–112, 156

Trade policy, 26, 133, 135–136, 163–164, 185–186

Transgender ideology, 114–115

Trans-Pacific Partnership (TPP), 163

Treason, x, 147, 206

Tribalism, 81–84, 86, 87, 90

Tribe, Laurence, 80–81

Truman, Harry, 136

Trump, Donald. *See also* Trump administration; *specific topics*
    alleged Russian collusion by, 24, 62–63, 73–74, 130, 131, 201, 203, 206, 210–211
    "American carnage" speech of, 38–40
    approval ratings for, xii
    attacks against, 190–191
    campaign promises kept by, 129–130, 162
    character quirks of, 125
    cultural leadership by, 180–182
    Democrats' hatred for and resistance to, xi–xii, 187–189
    election and campaign of, 1–3, 203
    El Paso mass shooting blamed on, 55–59, 62
    family history of, 185
    on gay marriage, 121
    inauguration of, 16, 37–40, 127–128
    as "Jew" of American politics, 59
    as leader of new Republican Party, xii–xiii
    legitimacy of election of, 15–17, 127–129, 193–194
    media attacks on, 23–24
    on "Muslim ban," 19
    personal attacks on, 4–5, 19–20
    political ambition of, 185–187
    political positions of, xi, 40–41
    as populist, 37–38
    presidential honeymoon period for, 16–17
    reelection campaign of, 67–69, 199–200
    rhetoric vs. policies as basis for judging, 137–141
    on the Squad, 94–96, 99–102
    as supporter of equal opportunities, 40–41
    supporters' defense of, xii
    Twitter feed of, 24–29 (*See also* Twitter)
    as "villain," 128–129
    and White House meeting with Kanye West, 11–12
    Zelensky's phone call with, 146, 151–155

Trump, Fred, 185

Trump, Friedrich, 185

Trump administration, 161–184, 188–189
    African Americans as beneficiaries of, 182–183
    border security policies, 173–174
    cooperation of, with impeachment inquiry, 156
    and corruption in Washington, 161–162
    and cultural leadership by Trump, 180–182
    defense of First Amendment by, 119–120
    economic growth under, 176–179
    on Equality Act, 116
    foreign policy under, 165–167, 170–173
    on Green New Deal, 111
    and Iran Nuclear Deal, 165–166
    judging the policies of, 137–141
    military funding under, 165–166
    on NATO contributions, 165
    trade policy under, 163–164
    on United Nations, 171–172
    on veterans' issues, 174–176
    war on Islamic terrorism under, 168–170

"Trump Clarification Syndrome" (Remnick), 132–137

Trump derangement syndrome, 123–141

and campaign promises kept, 129–130
in *The Death of Truth,* 124–131
and judging Trump's rhetoric vs. policies, 137–141
The New Yorker on, 132–137
in *New York Times,* 130–132
and questioning legitimacy of election, 127–129
Zakaria on, 123–124
"Trump's Anti-immigrant Rhetoric Looms Over El Paso Massacre," 56
"Trump's Timeline of Hate," 120
"Trump Urges Unity Vs. Racism," 58, 73
Turkish Empire, 97, 212
2020 census, 81
Twenty-fifth Amendment, 67
Twitter, 24–31, 33, 44, 58, 74, 94–95, 99–102, 135, 149, 155

Ukraine, 144–147, 152, 170
Unemployment, 8, 24, 26, 38, 105, 179, 186
United Nations, 141, 171–172, 210, 211
Unite the Right rally, 82
University of Louisville, 114, 115

VA Missions Act, 176
Vandenberg, Arthur, 70
Varadkar, Leo, 121
Veterans, 174–176
Veteran's Day Parade (New York), 174
Veteran's Heath Administration (VHA), 175
Virginia colony, 78, 209
Voting rights, 204

Wall, border, 20–21, 49, 173–174
Warren, Elizabeth, 14, 44, 48–49, 51, 54, 55, 85, 96, 109, 197–199

Wartime, partisan politics during, 69–71
Washington, D.C., 40
We Have Overcome (Hill), 45–46
Welfare system, in Green New Deal, 107, 110
"We're in a Permanent Coup" (Taibbi), 158–159
West, Kanye, 11–12
West Bank, 99–102, 173
Western Wall, Trump's visit to, 172
West Virginia, 2
What the Hell Do You Have to Lose? (Williams), 9–11
Whistleblower complaint, 147–151, 157–158
Whistleblower Protection Act, 157
White nationalism, xii, 4, 39–40, 54, 56–57, 75–76, 80–82
White racism, 73–75
White supremacy, 9, 10, 33, 57, 58, 74–75, 80–82, 96, 140, 188, 189, 194, 206
"Why Are Democrats Defending Sharpton?" (Loury), 43, 44
Wilkie, Robert, 176
Williams, Juan, 9–11
Wisconsin, 2, 3
Women, effects of Equality Act for, 117
Women's March, 15, 26, 101, 127
World War II, 17, 97, 111
WrestleMania, 25
Wright, Jeremiah, 5

Xenophobia, 6, 15, 23, 56, 76, 131, 190
Xi Jinping, 26, 139

Yanukovych, Viktor, 144

Zaid, Mark, 149
Zakaria, Fareed, 123–124
Zelensky, Volodymyr, 146, 151–155

About the Author

DAVID HOROWITZ is a conservative thinker and writer who has authored dozens of books over the course of his lifetime. He began his political career as one of the founders of the New Left in the 1960s and served as an editor of its largest magazine, *Ramparts*. As described in his bestselling autobiography *Radical Son* (1997), Horowitz was forced to confront some difficult truths about the political left after a close friend of his was murdered by the Black Panthers, and ultimately found a political and intellectual home as a conservative activist. Well-known conservative author and economist George Gilder described *Radical Son* as "the first great autobiography of his generation." In 2019 Horowitz published a second autobiographical memoir, *Mortality and Faith*.

Together with his friend Peter Collier, Horowitz authored three bestselling dynastic biographies: *The Rockefellers: An American Dynasty* (1976); *The Kennedys: An American Dream* (1984); and *The Fords: An American Epic* (1987). Looking back in anger at their days in the New Left, he and Collier wrote *Destructive Generation* (1989), a chronicle of their second thoughts about the sixties.

In 1988, David Horowitz founded the David Horowitz Freedom Center (originally named the Center for the Study of Popular Culture), a not-for-profit organization located in Sherman Oaks, California. The Center's mission is to defend free societies such as America and Israel, which are under attack by totalitarians both religious and secular, domestic and foreign.

Through his work at the Freedom Center, Horowitz has fought many important political battles, including exposing the deadly intentions of adherents to radical Islam and their stealth jihad in America, challenging left-wing indoctrination in our nation's K–12 public schools and universities, and advocating for colleges to withdraw funds from terrorist-affiliated campus organizations such as Students for Justice in Palestine. Horowitz is a frequent speaker at colleges and universities across the nation.

Horowitz's many published works include *The Art of Political War and Other Radical Pursuits*; *Unholy Alliance: Radical Islam and the American Left*; *The Professors: The 101 Most Dangerous Academics in America*; *Indoctrination U*; *One-Party Classroom, Reforming Our Universities, The New Leviathan* (with Jacob Laksin); *Party of Defeat* (with Ben Johnson) and *Radicals: Portraits of a Destructive Passion.*

Horowitz is also the author of *The Black Book of the American Left*, a nine-volume collection of his conservative writings over the past several decades, organized by topic. It is the most ambitious effort ever undertaken to define the Left and its agenda.

In addition to *Blitz: Trump Will Smash the Left and Win*, Horowitz has written three books with Humanix Books on the conflicts of the Trump Era. *Big Agenda: President Trump's Plan to Save America*, was published on Inauguration Day 2017 and was eleven weeks on the *New York Times'* best-seller list. *Dark Agenda: The War to Destroy Christian America*, was published in March 2019.

More Titles From Humanix Books You May Be Interested In:

Warren Buffett says:
"My friend, Ben Stein, has written a short book that tells you everything you need to know about investing (and in words you can understand). Follow Ben's advice and you will do far better than almost all investors (and I include pension funds, universities and the super-rich) who pay high fees to advisors."

In his entertaining and informative style that has captivated generations, beloved *New York Times* bestselling author, actor, and financial expert Ben Stein sets the record straight about capitalism in the United States — it is not the "rigged system" young people are led to believe.

Dr. Mehmet Oz says:
"*SNAP!* shows that personalities can be changed from what our genes or early childhood would have ordained. Invest the 30 days."

New York Times bestselling author Dr. Gary Small's breakthrough plan to improve your personality for a better life! As you read *SNAP!* you will gain a better understanding of who you are now, how others see you, and which aspects of yourself you'd like to change. You will acquire the tools you need to change your personality in just one month — it won't take years of psychotherapy, self-exploration, or re-hashing every single bad thing that's ever happened to you.

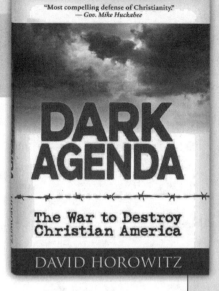